THE WORLD OF
FALCONRY

H. SCHLEGEL
J.A. VERSTER DE WULVERHORST

THE WORLD OF FALCONRY

COMPLETED BY A STUDY OF FALCONRY TODAY
IN THE ARAB WORLD

THE VENDOME PRESS
NEW YORK · PARIS · LAUSANNE

DISTRIBUTED BY THE VIKING PRESS, NEW YORK CITY

Distributed by The Viking Press
625 Madison Avenue
New York, New York 10022

Distributed in Canada by Viking Penguin

ISBN 0-86565-004-7
Library of Congress Catalog Card no. 80-51189

Printed in Switzerland

Contents

Preface

For centuries, man has enjoyed a rare partnership with certain birds of prey. An extraordinary relationship can be achieved between the most fearless and courageous of living creatures, the hawks, falcons, and eagles, and the falconer, who succeeds in controlling the natural instincts of these predators to serve his own ends. How does this strange partnership – for partnership it is, for these birds of prey cannot be domesticated by man – come about? This book tells the history and the methods used, from the earliest times until today, to establish this fragile bond between man and bird.

Falconry and hawking have a long and noble history. Their origins stretch back into the mists of antiquity, back to the Mesopotamian empires. Before the days of accurate weapons, man enlarged his possibilities for successful hunting by employing trained birds, so much faster and more accurate than a sling or arrow, to capture his prey. Starting perhaps as a necessity, falconry developed into a sport, with elaborate rules that reflected the chivalry of the middle ages. With the development of accurate firearms, falconry declined, aided by the increased settlement and enclosures that marked more settled times. But there has always been, as there is today, a band of enthusiasts who have kept alive this most difficult form of hunting. Today, more than ever, the sport is alive, in Arab countries, from whence came much of the technical progress, in America, where the vast spaces and the availability of both prey and the birds to catch it have enabled the sport to grow steadily, and in Europe, where despite the difficulties imposed by legislation, enclosure, and modern agricultural methods, a select band of enthusiasts still maintains the high standards handed down from their ancestors. But beware! Falconry is not for dilettanti, and demands especial qualities from whoever would seek to establish a partnership with a wild creature that refuses to be tamed. Time, patience, and a deep understanding and knowledge of his falcon are required, together with an almost instinctive sympathy, in order to make a success of this most demanding of sports.

This book sets out in detail the requirements for the taking, training, and flying of hawks and falcons. The heart of the book is the classic treatise written by two nineteenth-century falconers, who practised their sport with the Anglo-Dutch Society for Falconry at Loo, Holland. The original magnificent colour plates which illustrated this rare book have been faithfully reproduced, showing the birds used, and the furniture and equipment needed to train and handle them. To this has been added a history of the sport from its origins until today, illustrated by contemporary and modern illustrations and photographs. The East, where the sport still flourishes, has not been neglected, and the age-old methods of the Arabs are shown as they are still practised today. Here then is the background to this very special sport, which is both picturesque to the onlooker and countrylover, and fascinating to the sportsman and hunter.

T.R.C.

the origins of falconry

If we glance through the books that have been written on the subject of falconry – and they are many – we shall notice at once that opinions on the origins of the sport and its subsequent history are highly contradictory. The earliest reference that has been handed down to us is to be found in a Japanese work entitled *Extract from writings on falconry, both ancient and modern.* This tells of a grand hawking expedition which took place in the land of Tsu, in the country of Jun Meng, to the north of Lake Tong-ting in China (the present-day province of Hunan), and which was attended by the King of Tsu, Wen Wang. According to the documentary evidence, this monarch reigned from 689 to 675 B.C., which supports the belief that the tradition of hawking in the Far East is a very ancient one. We find, too, a reference to falcons having been sent to Japan from Korea in the year 247 A.D., although it would seem that the sport was not taken up there to any great extent for another hundred years or so.

The earliest writer in the western world to deal with the subject of hawking is Ctesias the Cnydian. Describing the country and customs of the pygmies, a mysterious people inhabiting some part of central Asia, Ctesias says, 'They hunt the fox and wolf, not with hounds, but with crows, kites, rooks, and eagles.' This remark must refer to hawking, and it comes at the beginning of a more detailed passage – preserved, not in the fragments by Ctesias himself that have come down to us, but in the writings of Aelian (c. 220 A.D.), who says: 'The Indians hunt the hare and fox in the following manner. They do not use hounds, but bring up the young of eagles, crows and kites, and train them for the taking of game. To this end, they let slip a tame hare or fox, having first tied to its tail a piece of meat; the birds are then released, and pursue the animal with all the speed they can muster in order to pounce on the bait, which they are then given as a reward for their obedience. Having been trained in this curious manner, they are then sent in pursuit of mountain hares and wild foxes, which they fly after eagerly in the hope of obtaining the usual reward. Having killed the quarry, they carry it to their master, and are then given, not the hoped-for

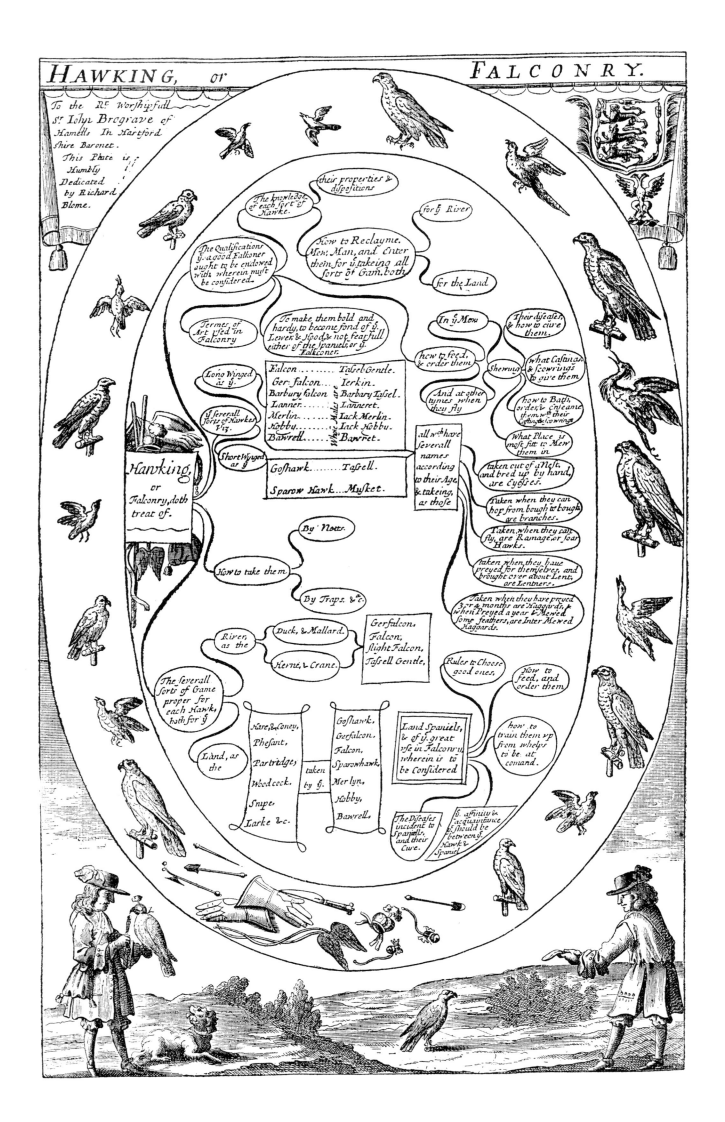

To the R.t Worshipfull S.r Iohn Brograve of Hamells In Hartford Shire Baronet. This Plate is Humbly Dedicated by Richard Blome.

their properties & dispositions

The knowledge of each sort of Hawke.

for y.e River

How to Reclayme. Men: Man, and Enter them, for y.e takeing all sorts of Game, both

for the Land

The Qualifications y.t a good Falkoner ought to be endowed with wherein must be considered.

Termes of Art used in Falconry

To make them bold and hardy, to become fond of y.e Lewer, & Hood, & not fearfull either of the Spaniels, or y.e Falconer.

In y.e Mew

Their diseases & how to cure them.

how to feed, & order them

Sheming

what Castings & scowrings to give them

Long Winged as y.e

Falcon . . . . Tassel Gentle.
Ger: falcon . . . . . Ierkin.
Barbury falcon . . Barbary Tassel.
Lanner . . . . Lanneret.
Merlin . . . . Iack Merlin.
Hobby . . . . Iack Hobby.
Bawrell . . . . Bawret.

Whose Males are

And at other tymes when they fly

how to Bath, order, & cnseane them w.th their Castin, & scowring

Of severall sorts of Hawkes Viz.

Short Winged as y.e

Goshawk . . . . Tassell.

Sparow Hawk . . . Musket.

all w.ch have severall names according to their Age, & takeing, as those

What Place is most fitt to Mew them in

Hawking or Falconry, doth treat of.

taken out of a Nest, and bred up by hand, are Eysses.

Taken when they can hop from bough to bough are branches.

By Netts.

Taken, when they can fly, are Ramage, or soar Hawks.

How to take them

taken when they haue preyed for themselves, and brought over about Lent, are Lentners.

By Traps, &.c

River, as the

Duck, & Mallard.

Gerfalcon, Falcon; flight Falcon, Tassell Gentle.

Taken when they have preyed 3, or 4, months are Haggards, when Preyed a year & Mewed some feathers, are Inter Mewed Haggards.

Herne, & Crane.

Rules to Choose good ones.

How to feed, and order them.

The severall sorts of Game proper for each Hawk, both for y.e

Hare, & Coney,
Phesant,
Partridge,
Woodcock,
Snipe,
Larke &c.

Goshawk,
Gerfalcon,
Falcon,
Sparowhawk,
Merlyn,
Hobby,
Bawrell.

Land Spaniels, & of y.e great use in Falconry wherein is to be Considered

how to train them up from whelps to be at comand.

Land, as the

taken by y.e

The Diseases incident to Spaniels, and their Cure.

y.e affinity & acquaintance y.t should be between y.e Hawk, & Spaniel.

Miniature from one of the earliest treatises on falconry to be written in the French language, 'Le Livre du Roy Modus et de la Royne Ratio', dating from the beginning of the fourteenth century.

meat, but the entrails of the animal killed.' Here is a plain description of hawking practice, from which we may assume that the sport must have been practised in central Asia at least as early as 400 B.C., when Ctesias was writing. It does, however, appear to show that hawking was not at that epoch known in India and Persia, for Ctesias was himself a native of Persia and court physician to Shah Artaxerxes Mnemon. The accounts of the expeditions of Alexander the Great contain no mention of hawking either, so perhaps we should conclude that it was not practised by any of the peoples he conquered, and that the people who did practise it at that period dwelt somewhere to the north of the countries that fell under his sway. The assumption that India knew nothing of the sport is confirmed, albeit negatively, by Sanskrit literature, which contains many references to various forms of hunting, including the hunting of the gazelle, but not to hunting with birds of prey. Nor do we find, among the wealth of sculptures adorning Indian and Persian monuments, any depicting hawks or hawking; and though in Egyptian sculpture there are representations of other forms of hunting, again there is none of hawking. Horapollo does not mention the sport, although he often speaks of the falcon as a bird sacred to the ancient Egyptians. Apart from the passages from Ctesias and Aelian we have already mentioned, there are no references to hawking in classical literature, from the earliest period up the fourth century. We can only assume that neither the Greeks nor the Romans were familiar with the sport; and this seems to hold good for the various peoples who traded with the Romans or were colonized by them. The Greeks and Romans, fond as they always were of anything remarkable, would surely have written extensively on the subject if they had had any knowledge of it; and they would not have described, in such terms as to suggest it was an odd, outlandish custom, the hunting of small birds as practised in Thrace. Nor would Ctesias and Aelian, in the description of the hawking practices of central Asia which we have quoted, have used expressions that testify to their ignorance in the matter.

We cannot, then, say with certainty at what date falconry came into being. Its beginnings are shrouded in obscurity. Nor can we pronounce upon the date at which it was introduced into the various countries where it later flourished. It does not seem to have been known in Europe until the beginning of the fourth century, under Constantine; and unfortunately Firmicus, the earliest writer to refer to the sport, offers no opinion about its possible origins. So we do not know if it was introduced by way of western Asia and the peoples with whom both Greeks and Romans had regular trading relations, or if it was the Huns who were responsible for spreading its secrets and skills westwards into Europe.

The exact dates at which hawking was introduced among the peoples of Persia, Arabia, and India, are no less elusive. Firdausi, in the tenth century, names Shah Thimuraz, third king of Persia, as the first monarch to hunt with the cheetah and the falcon; but we do not know when this ruler lived, Firdausi being an unreliable guide, not only moving the period he mentions back in time as far as 3000 B.C. but making several kings of Persia rule for a hundred, on occasion even a thousand, years. Demiry and Ghitrif Hijaj state that the Caliph Harun al-Rashid hunted with hawks, but it does not appear probable that the Arabs were acquainted with the sport before the spread of the Arab conquests during the seventh century. As far as India is concerned, it seems likely that hawking was introduced there by the Muslim invaders in the tenth and eleventh centuries. At the time of the Spanish Conquest, the reigning dynasty in Mexico hunted with birds of prey; and it is more than possible that Asia, again, was responsible for introducing the sport into the New World. But if we try to fix upon a date, we must once again fall back on mere guesswork.

The art of falconry was probably invented, very far back in time, among the nomad people who wander the wastes of central Asia, and spread thence eastwards through China to Japan and the New World, and westwards through India, Persia, western Asia, Europe and north Africa. We have no evidence of hawking being practised in peninsular India, nor in Malaya, New Holland, North America, or Africa south of the Mediterranean littoral. Nor can we say at what date it finally arrived in Europe. On some occasion or other, Gregory of Tours is said to have addressed these words to Merovius, the fifth-century King of the Franks: 'Come, sire, bid them saddle our horses; let us take our hawks and our hounds, and let us go hunt and be merry.' There is also a fifth-century epigram, aimed at a fat falconer who let his hawks starve, which says he should rather have let them feed on his own excess of flesh than allow them to die for want of meat through his own meanness.

By this time, falconry was widespread and popular in France and several other countries, if we may judge by the laws passed during the early Middle Ages to regulate hawkers and their hawks. One such law, found in the Burgundian penal code, clearly reveals the cruel harshness of the contemporary laws of the chase. It says that a man found guilty of the theft of a hunting hawk shall pay six sous to the bird's owner; or that the bird shall remove from the buttocks of the said thief six ounces of flesh.

This drawing of a falcon on a moveable perch is taken from the Emperor Frederic II of Hohenstaufen's celebrated *Art of Falconry* (*De Arte Venandi cum Avibus*), written in the thirteenth century.

This Assyrian bas-relief, now in the Louvre, shows that hawking was known to the inhabitants of ancient Mesopotamia.

A superb contemporary portrait of Federico di Capdilista, mounted on his destrier with hawk on fist. He died on Crusade at the age of 22.

The Lombards had a law which forbade 'the giving of a sword or a sparrowhawk, in ransom or in bond.' The clergy, as ardent in their love of hawking as the laity, had to be expressly discouraged, in the sixth century and at intervals thereafter, from owning falcons. The ban was renewed by St Boniface; it formed part of the rule of the Knights Templars; yet as late as 1303 the Synod of Auch found it necessary to forbid archdeacons to take their hounds and hawks round with them on diocesan visits. The art of training hounds and hawks was one of the very first lessons in the bringing-up of little Blanchardin, Charlemagne's son. King Cardoman kept four venerers, in charge of the royal kennels, and one falconer, who looked after the royal mews. They were subordinate to three senior officers of the Household: the Seneschal, the Butler, and the Constable, and were in charge of the entire hunt, and all that pertained to it, including the acquisition of new hawks on the king's behalf.

Falconry appears to have been a less popular sport than hunting up to the time of the crusades, despite having been practised in Europe since at least the fourth century; but in consequence of the crusades it was to receive fresh impetus from the orient. We are told in the work on falconry[1] by Frederick II, Holy Roman Emperor, that the Arabs were at that period much more skilful practitioners of the art than any other nation, and it is to the Arabs and their writings that we owe the knowledge that did so much to develop the art and spread its popularity. During the crusades, indeed, hawking rose in favour to such an extent that it began to usurp somewhat the position held by hunting in the popular favour. The jealousy excited by this rivalry between falconers and hunting men gave rise to much ill feeling and many outright squabbles between the two

[1] *De Arte Venandi cum Avibus*, c. 1247.

The Moghul princes of India were great devotees of falconry, and many illustrations of the chase were made for them. Here a cavalier is about to fly his hawk at the cranes and ducks in the background. His hawks carry a halsband about their necks.

factions, squabbles which continued to burst out now and then even when, in the days of Louis XIV, hunting regained its old pre-eminence.

As the indispensable accessory of a gentleman, or gentlewoman, a hawk may often be found in old pictures (my lord or my lady having sat for their portrait with hawk on fist), in miniatures, on seals, and on monuments. Noblemen sometimes acquired privileges which in a few cases led to strange abuses. The Seigneurs of Chastelas, for example, had the right to sit, when they so desired, among the canons of the church of Auxerre, girt with their sword, clad in a surplice, wearing a plumed hat, the amice, or clerical cape, over their arm, and their hawk on their fist. This privilege was accorded to the members of this influential family in the year 1423. The treasurer of the same church enjoyed the right of attending divine service on feast-days with his hawk on his fist. His right was contested by his brother canons, but had to be confirmed, largely because the treasurer of the church of Nevers enjoyed a similar privilege. The following ordinance refers to rights granted to the Seigneur of Sassay and the curé of Ezy: 'The Sieur de Sassay may hear mass said by the curé of Ezy (or another) in the church of Our Lady of Evreux, before the high altar, Whenever him pleaseth; and the same lord or curé may fly his goshawk and tiercel over the whole diocese of Evreux, with six spaniels and two hounds, and the said lord may carry and set down his hawk on the corner of the high altar wherever seemeth to him the best and nearest place. The said lord or curé may say mass booted and spurred in the said church of Our Lady of Evreux, with drum beating instead of the organ.' Hawks were, as we shall see in a later chapter, imported from Iceland, Norway, Greece, the Barbary coast, and many other countries, even America; and exorbitantly high prices were often paid for them. The different species of hawks were valued in accordance with their respective hunting qualities, and the different grades of hawk were matched to the appropriate rank in society. The ruling that set out these nice distinctions may be found in many English books.[1] The emperor was allotted the eagle, vulture, and kite; the gyrfalcon was assigned to kings; the falcon gentle to princes; the falcon of the loch to dukes; the peregrine to earls; the buzzard to barons; the saker to knights; the lanner to esquires; the merlin to ladies; the hobby to young men; the sparrowhawk to priests; the goshawk to yeomen; the kestrel to servants. Kings, in their ceremonial entrances and progresses, used always to be preceded by their retinue of falcons with their falconers, and this custom may still be found, even today, on grand ceremonial occasions such as coronations.[2]

To sum up, it is wellnigh impossible for us, today, to conceive of the vastly important part played by falconry in the life of our ancestors. In those departed days, a knowledge of the art was absolutely essential to the upbringing of a gentleman. That is the explanation, too, of the large number of books which have found their way into print on the subject, and the numerous editions most of these have gone through.

[1] The original is the *Boke of St. Albans,* 1486.
[2] In 1900 the hereditary Grand Falconer of England was the Duke of St. Albans.

Falcons were part of everyday life for everyone, not only the rich and aristocratic. They even appeared on playing cards, as in this set belonging to the owners of Schloss Ambras in the Tyrol.

A sixteenth-century engraving that might be entitled the *Pleasures of the Countryside*. The falconer is about to fly his bird, his lure in his right hand, to the musical accompaniement of the hunter with the hound. Above, the falcons ring up after heron, and in the background, Strephon and Amaryllis dally in the shade, while the sheep get lost.

17

Robert Cheseman, falconer to King Henry VIII,
painted by Hans Holbein the Younger about 1625.

the language of falconry

Hawking, like hunting, has its own vocabulary, and this must be mastered at the start if we are to make anything of the books written on the subject. The study of the terms used, however, raises more difficulties than might at first be supposed. Their meaning has sometimes altered, under the vicissitudes of time and place, so that a word may sometimes be found to mean different things to different writers. France has been fortunate in that several learned and distinguished writers on hawking have been French, with the result that the French terms employed are both more numerous and more widely-known than those of other tongues.

Hawks are given different names, not only according to their sex, their age, and sometimes to the season in which they taken, but also according to the kind of hawking for which they are to be used. Male hawks are known as *tiercels,* or tercels; we would say, for example, the tiercel goshawk, or the tiercel falcon. But the word tiercel is not used for the male of the saker falcon, which is called the *sakret*; nor of the lanner, which is the *lanneret*; nor of the sparrowhawk, which is the *musket*.[1] The female birds are known simply by the name of the species to which they belong.

Young birds taken from the nest are called *eyasses,* or eyass hawks; a young bird which has learnt to hop from branch to branch, but which has not yet the strength of wing to enable him to escape the would-be hunter, is called a *brancher,* or *bowiser*. Birds taken at the period of the migration, or passage, are known as *passagers,* or *passage hawks,* so one would say 'a passage lanner' or 'a passage goshawk'. The name 'passage hawk' is given more especially, however, to common falcons taken during the migration, and in applying it to that species, we usually use the word 'peregrine'. [2] A further distinction may be drawn by using the word *lantiner*[3] for passage hawks taken in spring, as opposed to *peregrine* in the narrower sense of hawks taken during the peregrination of the last three months of the year. Before the first moult, while still in their immature plumage,

[1]The firearm takes its name from him.
[2]Passage being a kind of peregrination, or pilgrimage.
[3]As in *lent.*

hawks are known as *sore-hawks* [1], sore, as in *sorrel,* or *red-hawks.* Birds which have moulted and assumed their adult plumage are known as *haggards* if captured thus from the wild. If they moult in captivity, they are known as *intermewed* hawks.

The number of years a hawk has spent in captivity may also be indicated by the number of its moults. A hawk in its second year would be 'an intermewed peregrine', 'an intermewed goshawk', 'an intermewed saker'; and one might say of a hawk that it had been through eight moults, meaning that it was eight years old.

Falconers have their own special names for the different parts of the bird's body – names unknown in ordinary, everyday speech and in scientific terminology as well. The following are the ones it is most important to know. The waxy membrane which covers the base of the beak in birds of prey is known to falconers as the *cere.* The toes are called the *petty singles*; the longest toe is the *long single.* The legs of a hawk from the thigh to the foot are known as the *arms*; the foot is known as the *hand*; but this latter term only applies to the true falcons, so that we should say the *hand* of a falcon, but the *foot* of a hawk. The stomach is called the *panell.* The wings are known as the *sails.* The large feathers of the forearm, the flight-feathers, are the *remiges,* of which the primaries, ten in number, are attached to the bones of the hand; these feathers differ in length according to the species, and have different names. The outermost primary in the wing is the *sarcel*; the seventh primary is the *beam* feather.[2] In falcons, the first primary is the longest; in hawks, the fourth. The bastard wing consists of the little feathers attached to the bone corresponding to the thumb.

The term *train* is used by many writers on falconry to mean the tail of the bird; other writers consider that it should only apply to short-winged hawks. The two centre feathers of the tail are known as the *deck-feathers.* The dark bars across the tails of birds of prey are commonly called the *tail-bands.* The part of the throat known in anatomy as the oesophagus is called the crop. If a hawk is in poor health, and unable to digest her food, or *put over her crop,* she may be *crop-bound.* The excreta of falcons are called *mutes*; dropping them is known as *muting,* or *slicing. Slicings* are the excreta of hawks. The term *eyrie* is used for the nest of a bird of prey, and also for the makeshift nest used for housing eyasses.

The following terms refer to the training and handling of birds of prey. *Making* a hawk means training her. Giving a hawk a *gorge,* or a *full gorge,* or *crop,* means feeding her as much as she can eat. One may also say 'half-gorge', 'a small crop', or 'quarter crop', etc. according to the amount of meat given. When a hawk pulls a beakful of meat, this is called a *bechin*; 'giving her a few bechins' would mean allowing her to eat only a few morsels. If hawks are too fat and heavy from overfeeding, they are said to be *in high condition* or *high,* and it is then necessary to give them less food than usual

[1] Sore, as in *sorrel.*

[2] The primaries are numbered from 1 to 10 from the outer edge inwards, the first primary being the one furthest from the body when the wing is spread.

The illustrations to the *Art of Falconry* show the method of taking falcons off the perch, unfastening their leashes with the traditional falconer's knot. A further illustration shows the birds on the block, with the leash being taken through the varvels and fastened to the ring. Finally, a horse trained to stand still is needed when mounting from the nearside with a falcon on the fist.

for a time, so as to 'lower them', or 'reduce their condition'. If, on the other hand, the birds are in low condition, it is necessary to increase their daily rations to bring them back into condition again. The pair of pigeon's or poultry wings, with meat attached, which is used to call the bird to the fist, is known as the *lure*. Feeding a hawk from the lure means that she is allowed to pull a few bechins from the meat on the lure. The pieces of bone, fur, and feathers which used to be given to a hawk to help her digest the butcher's meat which forms her daily diet were called *castings*; consequently one said 'to give castings'. Sometimes a little meat might be put to the castings to help the bird to swallow them. *Imping* a feather means mending a broken or damaged feather with an *imping-needle* and a similar feather preserved for the purpose. *Seeling*[1] a hawk means sewing up her eyelids in order to prevent her from seeing. *Weathering* a hawk means putting her outside, to take the sun and air. Hawks are *carried on the fist*. The action by which the hawk is released from the fist to fly at the quarry is called *casting* or *slipping* the hawk. The expression to *fly at bolt* means to fly from the fist, when flying short-winged hawks. Letting a hawk fly high up while the dog or falconers flush the quarry for her is known as *waiting on*. When a hawk perches in a tree, she is said to *take stand*. A *carrier* is a hawk which carries the quarry away. In falconry language, a bird which seizes the quarry in her feet is said to *bind to* it, or *truss to* it. To call a hawk back to her owner one uses the lure, or a pigeon on a line: this is known as *calling to the lure*, or using live lure.[2] Short-winged are not called to the lure, but called, or whistled, to the fist. The captive birds used for training the hawks, and held on a line during training sessions, are known as *bagged* or *captive quarry*; which may be a *bagged pigeon,* a *bagged partridge,* or cock, or heron, or kite, etc.[3] One says of a hawk that she is *manned,* or manned to the fist, when she will stay quietly on the fist without *bating*. When her training is complete, she is said to be *made.*

Falconry is the art of training and controlling birds of prey. A falconer, strictly speaking, trains falcons. An austringer trains hawks, such as goshawk and sparrowhawk. Falcons, being trained to fly to the lure, are known in consequence as *hawks of the lure*. Hawks are trained to fly to the fist, and are thus known as *hawks of the fist*. Hawks of the lure are the long-winged hawks, with high, soaring flight. Hawks of the fist are the short-winged hawks, low in flight. Hawking is the hunting of game, either feathered or furred, using trained hawks. Hawking proper, in former days, was the flying of long-winged hawks at quarry, and in particular at heron and kite; game-hawking was the flying of either long-winged or short-winged hawks at game, such as hare, partridge, duck, and so on. To *fly,* in the language of falconry, has the same meaning as 'hunt', so that one may say, 'to fly kite', 'to fly partridge', or 'this falcon has flown heron', etc. The noun *flight* is used in a similar way, so one may use the expression, 'a flight

[1] Seeling is illegal in Gt Britain.
[2] Using live birds either as bait or for training is illegal in Gt Britain.
[3] This practice is illegal in Gt Britain.

at heron' – or crows, etc. Hawking, like shooting, can be further divided into game-hawking, grouse-hawking, partridge-hawking, and so on. Falconers usually say, 'to fly peregrines, goshawks, sparrow-hawks', rather than 'to hunt with peregrines', etc.

Few people may be aware that a falconer mounts his horse on the off, or right, side, because he carries his hawk on his left fist. We might note here that the expression 'to mount falconer-fashion', sometimes heard among horsemen, means to mount on the right, or using the right foot.

Prairie falcon from America. This very efficient bird will take quail, partridge and pheasant.

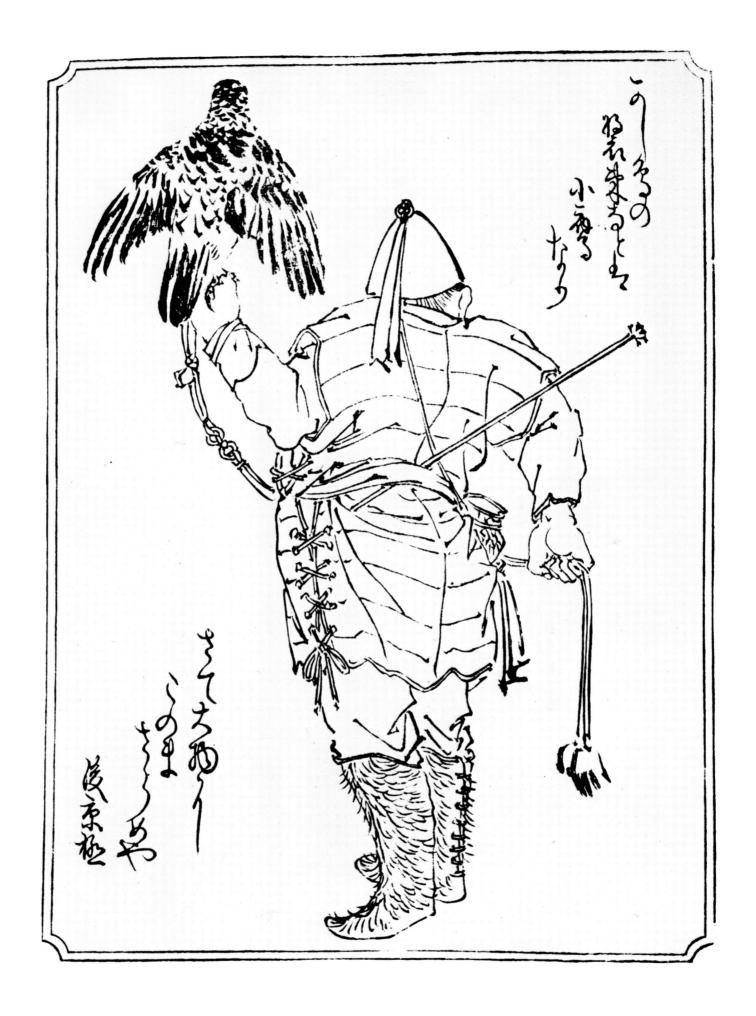

このうまの
ねれ来るとて
小こ弯る
なりの

もてきゆり
このま
ましや
後京極

24

the falconer's furniture and appliances

The various tools and implements used in falconry being depicted in the present work in the most exact detail, we do not propose to give here a minute description of them. It will suffice if we go through them briefly, adding such observations as may be necessary to make the reader familiar with their names, properties, and uses.

The short leather straps, or thongs, put round the feet of birds used in hawking, in order to prevent them from flying away, are known as the *jesses*. Jesses are of two patterns, according to whether they are intended for the goshawk or for other birds of prey. They are composed of two main parts: the *jesses*, and the *leash*; which are connected by a third piece, the *swivel*. In the case of the goshawk there is a fourth piece, the *shortleash*, which comes between the jesses and the swivel, the jesses for the goshawk being furnished at their lower end with a thin brass ring. All these pieces of equipment vary in size according to the size of the bird they are to fit. The jesses are made of two pieces of leather of exactly similar shape; they are supple leather straps, which are tied round the bird's tarsi by means of a special knot. The swivel is composed of two metal rings, joined by a short neck or shank, upon which they can turn freely. The upper ring, or D. receives the long ends of the jess or shortleash; the leash is threaded through the lower ring. The shortleash is a leather band about two inches long, with a running knot at the end, which is tightened on the rings of a goshawk's jesses. The leash is a slender leather thong, about three feet in length, used for tying the hawks to their perch, or any other object. The *creance*, or *cranes*, is a long line which is attached to the leash during training in the field until such time as the bird may be trusted to fly free. The *bell* is attached to the hawk's left foot, above the jess, by a thin leather strap called the *bewit*. When tying the knot of the jess, a piece of wood shaped roughly like an awl is used to hold open the slit cut in the leather through which the pointed end of the jess is pushed. For tying on the bell, a thick piece of wire may answer the purpose, filed to a point at one end and bent into a circle at the other. To quieten a bird which constantly bates when

A Japanese falconer, engraved by Kyosai about 1870. The long jesses, the swivel, and the leash form part of his equipment. From *The Mirror of Hawks*. Meat was kept in the small lacquer box whose lid the falconer tapped to draw the bird's attention. The long stick on the falconer's back is a frisfass, a piece of wisteria teased out at the end and used to stroke the bird and so avoid spoiling its plumage by hand stroking.

on the cadge, the *brail* is used, to hobble the right wing. This is a thin, soft, leather thong, with a slit in it through which the upper part of the wing may be drawn, confining it.

The *hood* used to cover the heads of hawks of the lure varies in size according to the size of the bird it is made for. The ordinary hood is surmounted by a tuft of feathers. The hood used for newly-caught hawks is plain, and made of thinner, softer leather than the ordinary hood; it is known as a *rufter*. Putting the hood on the bird is known as *hooding*; taking it off is called *striking the hood* (when the braces are loosened) and *unhooding* (when it is removed). The wooden block on which the hood is shaped must be made with great precision; for if the hood is too loose the bird will claw it off, whereas, if it is tight, it may injure the bird's head or break her feathers. The *lure* is a dummy, or imitation, pigeon; it may be fashioned out of a flat piece of wood, rounded at the front, forked at the back, covered with leather, and having on each side a pair of pigeon's wings, laid close and stuck down. The thongs fixed to each side of the lure, just above the fork, are for tying on the bait – that is, a piece of raw meat. The eye-hook fixed to the front is to take the *lure-line*, which is used to swing the lure, and which, looped up for carrying, is slung over the falconer's right shoulder so that it hangs down on his left-hand side.

The *hawking-bag,* or hawking-pouch, is a kind of game-pouch with two compartments, made of green canvas and provided with a leather strap which buckles round the hip; it is worn on the right-hand side. One of its pockets is for carrying the box of meat, the creance, the jesses, the knife, the pincers, and any other things which may come in useful when training or out hawking; the other pocket, which may be closed by means of a drawstring, is for carrying the pigeons which are to be used as live lure, or bagged quarry for training.

The *cadge* is a sort of portable perch, or doolie, on which the hawks are tied for the journey out to the field; the boy who carries the cadge is known as the *cadger,* or *cadge-boy.* A piece of coarse linen, or *sock,* is also used for putting round a newly-caught hawk; this has a wide hem, or pocket, on each side, and is about a foot square, wider at the bottom than the top, and with two tapes, about a foot and a half in length, stitched to the back. The wings are inserted into the pockets, and the feet tied with

A French engraving of a model mews, consisting of the falconer's lodge (centre), and covered screen perches for the birds down each side of the court. Fig. 1 shows the falconer carrying a cadge; fig. 2 turf blocks for weathering; fig. 3 the screen perches. Nextdoor, on the right, seems to be a pigeon loft.

A busy scene in the falconer's lodge. Fig. 1 depicts a falconer carrying hoods; fig. 2 another preparing feathers for imping; while figs 3 and 4 show a falconer and his assistant about to cast the bird to imp new feathers.

26

fig. 2.   fig. 1.

fig. 1.   fig. 2.   b   fig. 3.   fig. 4.

f

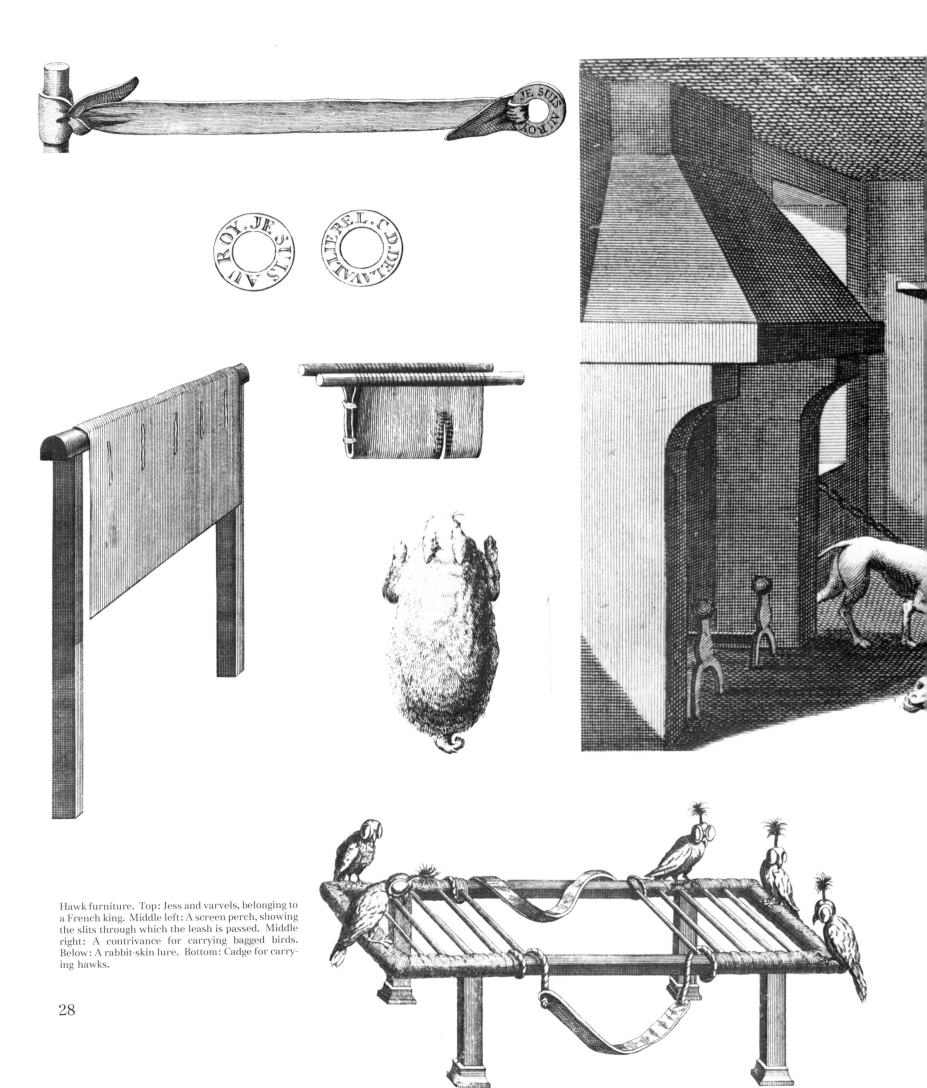

Hawk furniture. Top: Jess and varvels, belonging to a French king. Middle left: A screen perch, showing the slits through which the leash is passed. Middle right: A contrivance for carrying bagged birds. Below: A rabbit-skin lure. Bottom: Cadge for carrying hawks.

28

Falconers preparing food for their charges. In fig. 1, a falconer bleeds a pigeon over a bowl of minced meat; fig. 2, another falconer carves a leg of mutton before chopping it. Also shown are (a) a leg of mutton; (b) a slab of beef; (c) a chopping block; (d) a carving knife; (e) a bowl; (f) a pigeon's wing for tirings; (g) eggs for adding to the food; (h and k), stones for rangle; (l) water jug; (n) basin for heating water in winter; (o, p and q) a greyhound, a spaniel and a mastiff.

Left: A hood, seen from front and rear, and showing the plume and the braces for opening and closing it.

29

the tapes so that the bird is pinioned and incapable of movement when put down on the ground. A tin box is used to hold the portion of finely-chopped meat which forms the bird's daily rations. The imping-needle, used for imping feathers, is made of hard steel and is triangular in section. It is about an inch long, and pointed at each end, so as to slide smoothly into the shaft of the feather needing repair. Imping-needles may conveniently be kept in an ordinary needle-case. For the operation known as seeling, which we propose to go into more fully in a later chapter, ordinary sewing-needles and fine cotton thread are used. The pincers and the knife are used, the former for blunting the talons and beak, the latter for *coping,* or paring, the beak when overgrown. The room in which the hawks' perches are placed is known as the hawk-house, or *mews.*[1] In order to prevent the herons used during training from striking out at the hawks with their beaks, these are muzzled with a *beak-shield* made of two sections of an elder twig about an inch long, bound together with thread.

[1] Formerly used for the moulting-quarters, from the French *muer* – to moult.

Right: Lithograph from the *Traité de Fauconnerie,* Schlegel and Wulverhorst, showing various items of furniture. Top centre: the lure, flanked by two dutch hoods. Below: a falconer's bag, showing both sides. The reverse side is provided with a compartment closed by a drawstring for carrying live pigeons to serve to the falcons. Bottom: Another dutch hood, flanked by two rufter hoods.

Method of transporting falcons by car. It is not always necessary to hood them.

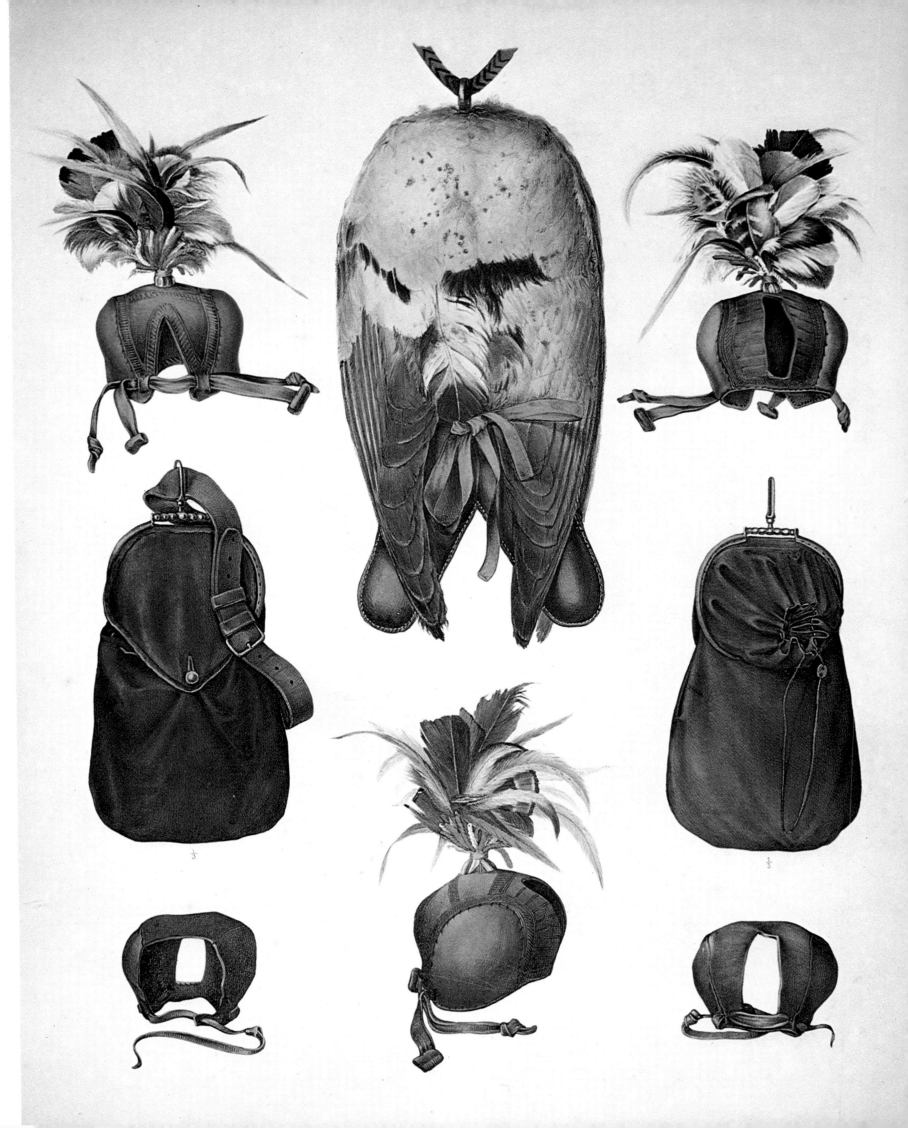

the birds used for hawking

Although a large number of diurnal birds of prey may be trained to fly at game, and although attempts have been made in the past to train other species besides, such as crows and shrikes, only a small number of species possess that combination of qualities which make them superlatively good at the work. It is widely believed that these qualities depend largely on the degree of mental development that a particular species has attained, or on its innate courage; but anyone who has had anything to do with hawks must have observed that such differences – if, indeed, they are there at all – are so slight that they are hardly worth bearing in mind when making a selection of birds. It will be found that the varying capacity for obedience shown by a hawk depends solely on the docility or obstinacy of temperament displayed by the species or the individual; that the level of courage shown may well be higher among the different birds of a single species than among the total number of birds in other species; and that courage on its own is of no service if the bird lacks the strong feet and powerful flight that can put what courage she has to good effect.

If we examine the real motives which lead a hawk to accept manning and learn to obey her master's commands, we shall very soon admit that to attain this result we need merely arouse and then satisfy, alternately, her instinctive needs, and that the level of the bird's brain development does not matter a fig. Lastly, we shall see that for successful hawking we can only use those species which nature has provided with the strength of wing and foot necessary to catch and grip their prey, and whose physical prowess is matched by their courage. It follows that, of the species that are endowed with such qualities, we shall do best if we simply select the biggest. It next becomes clear that we shall be wasting our time if we try to hunt with species – such as the kites, the buzzards, and the vultures – whose foot-formation renders them incapable of seizing an agile quarry; that species such as the harrier, whose feet are certainly better suited for the work, cannot be chosen either, because they are not fast enough on the

A falconer's assistant, or cadge boy, carrying the cadge. An eighteenth-century engraving by J. E. Riedinger.

33

wing; that species such as the kestrel, the redfooted falcon, etc., which are fast in flight but have smaller, weaker feet, must also be eliminated; and that even species such as the hobby and the sapphire falcon, which are very fast in flight and also have the right foot-formation, cannot be flown with success, as they do not possess the cunning or skill to use their feet to the best advantage when attacking their prey. And so, having learned from the numerous attempts which have been made over the years to train other sorts of birds of prey to fly at quarry, we have come in the end to use only those species in whom those characteristics we have described are most outstanding – provided, of course, that no other circumstances occur to detract from their usefulness, such as, for instance, the habits of the osprey, whose sole food is fish, and of the sea-eagles, who live entirely on fish and carrion. Eagles proper have been used only seldom for hawking, partly because of their rarity, but partly too because they are too heavy to carry on the fist, and because the large game we would hope to fly them at is not found here in Europe.

It will be seen from the above remarks that, having eliminated most of the European birds of prey, we are left with only a small number of species which are really suitable for hawking, and these are the larger falcons, the merlin, the goshawk, and the sparrowhawk. It was in consequence of the use of these species for hunting purposes that the age-old division of hawks into two categories originally arose – the categories corresponding to the families known to naturalists as the true falcons, and the hawks. The merlin belongs, as is well known, to the falcon family, whereas the goshawk and sparrowhawk belong, by reason of their essential characteristics, to the hawk family. This division of hawks into two classes is also to be found among several Asian peoples, from which we may deduce that falcons and hawks have been regarded throughout history and by many different nations as the hunting birds *par excellence.* The two classes are quite different, not only in their habits, but in a number of physical features, especially in their wing-formation; and as they are handled in quite a different manner both during training and in the field, it has happened that, over the years, several different expressions have arisen to indicate the differences between the two families, or classes, of birds. So we have the name 'hawk of the lure' for the falcon, and 'hawk of the fist' for the hawk. The former is a high-flying, the latter a low-flying, hawk. The art of falconry is divided into falconry proper, if falcons are flown, and hawking, if the birds flown are sparrowhawks and goshawks. The falcon is generally hooded; the hawk is not. Falcons have long wings, and are thus called the longwinged hawks, or long-wings. Hawks have short wings, and are known as short-winged hawks; and whereas falcons' eyes are dark, the eyes of hawks are yellow.

The species used in Europe for hawking are ten in number. They are, among the long-wings: the white falcon, the Iceland falcon, the gyrfalcon or gerfalcon, the saker, the lanner, the Alphanet or Tunisian lanner, the peregrine, and the merlin; among the short-wings: the goshawk and the sparrowhawk.

Lanner coming in to the lure at the Falconry Centre, Newent, England.

The long-winged hawks

The birds known among falconers as long-winged hawks all belong to the division of the falcon family traditionally known as the noble falcons. These form a large group, rich in species, widely distributed throughout the world. They have, in common with the other members of the falcon family, the lower mandible truncated at the tip and furnished with a notch on either side which corresponds to the feature known as the *tooth,* on each side of the upper mandible, behind which may be found a second notch, or *festoon,* which is more like a slight curve. They are strong, sturdy birds, with a muscular neck, a rather broad skull, strong feet, and long toes, provided underneath with large tubercles and armed with large, curving talons. The tarsi, covered in scales which are larger and more irregular

Goshawk coming in to the fist.

at the front, are feathered only on their front upper portion. The plumage of falcons is close and dense, the flight feathers being very straight and thick. The tail, always composed of twelve feathers, is of medium length and blunt, or slightly rounded, at the tip. The wings are tapering and when closed cover, in some species, two-thirds or three-quarters of the tail, in others its entire length. The first primary is sometimes slightly longer, sometimes slightly shorter than the third, but always shorter than the second, which is invariably the longest. This first feather is noticeably emarginated on the inner web for about the last quarter of its length; in the merlin this feature is found in the second primary. This species also has the outer webs of the second and third primaries notched, whereas in

The lanner, which is found over most of Africa, and is used in Morocco and Algeria.

37

the other falcons the second primary is the only one with a noticeable notch on the outer web. The iris of the eye is always a very dark brown. The cere, the orbits, and the feet are rather bright yellow in the adult birds, verging frequently on bluish or greenish; in the young birds these parts are generally pale bluish-green, often merging into yellow on the scales of the toes.

Falcons undergo one complete moult each year, which takes place towards the end of July and during August; but it is quite common, at the approach of the courting season, when the plumage has been damaged, for them to undergo a partial moult of a few isolated feathers on the neck, head, and under-parts; this local, partial moult, however, does not result in any change in the colouring of the plumage. The first general moult takes place when the bird is a year old, and the bird then acquires its perfect plumage, generally speaking more vivid in hue and more beautiful in its markings than the juvenile. The succeeding moults do not to any striking extent alter the colouring, except in the jack (male) merlin and to a lesser extent in the tiercel falcon, these changes being limited, generally, to an increased brightness in colour and narrower streakings on the under-parts. In immature birds of the same species the sexes are indistinguishable as to colour, this similarity persisting in the adult plumage, only the adult jack merlin displaying any difference in his plumage from the female. But where size is concerned, this equality ends – the male being, as in all birds of prey, up to a seventh or an eighth smaller than the female. The plumage of falcons is subject to enormous individual variation; but this variation (apart from that produced by the influence of atmosphere or weather) is limited to slight changes of shades in the colours, and slight differences in the shape and number of the streaks.

In the wild, long-winged hawks live exclusively on live prey, and almost always on birds; but the merlin will also eat a great many insects of every kind, if she can get nothing better. Falcons do not take sitting birds, either on the ground or in the branches of trees. Endowed with amazing strength, powerful wings, and feet so constructed that they can seize and bind to their prey, falcons will attack and kill the most agile of birds, taking them on the wing by stooping on them obliquely from a height. Having seized their prey in their feet, they carry it off, and, pitching either on the ground, or on a knoll, or any other convenient perch, such as a tree, they kill it at once, and tear into the flesh with their beak. Long-winged hawks live either singly or in pairs. They rear only one brood a year. They build their eyries either in crannies amongst rocks, or in trees or bushes, or sometimes even on the ground. The eggs, three or four in number, and a regular, rather rounded, oval in shape, are of a greenish-white generally freckled, closely or sparsely, with brown. When hatched, the young are covered in white down, which wears off and disappears as the true feathers, to which the down is attached, push through the skin. The first moult, as we have already noted, does not generally take place until the following year, and it is then that the adult plumage is assumed in more or less its perfect state.

Left: White tailed Sea Eagle. Right: Sparrowhawk.

The habitat chosen by the true falcons varies according to the different species and according to the season of the year. Some, during the breeding season, will haunt the forest, while others prefer the hills; a few, but a few only, come down to the open lowlands and moors where the cover is sparse, consisting of heather, bushes, and low shrubs. Their particular mode of attack leads them to seek their prey in open country, in clearings, along woodland rides and glades, or the adjacent fields and downland. At the approach of winter and winter's cold, most falcons migrate – some coming down from their high hills and forests to the moors, or to cultivated land, drawn by the abundance of game to be found there; they may then be found in the vicinity of humankind, taking up residence in old barns, or upon towers in the middle of towns, from whence they make forays against the denizens of local fowl-houses and poultry-yards. Certain species, especially those whose summer quarters are in cold countries, emigrate in winter to lands holding out the prospect of easier hunting, and may spend the colder months in places very remote from their usual haunts.

Top: White eyed Buzzard from India. Above: White bellied Sea Eagle from Asia. Left: Hodgson's Hawk-Eagle, Japan. Right: African Black Sparrow-hawk. Below: Immature lanner Falcon. Far right: Immature Goshawk.

Some species have in common a number of characteristics by which they may be distinguished from other species – which, again fall naturally into groups of their own; so the true falcons may be divided into several classes, or sub-divisions. We propose, in the following pages, to describe only those species to be found in Europe.

The first of these sub-divisions includes the large falcons whose tails are long enough to protrude some way beyond the tips of the wings when the wings are folded. Their feet, though strong and well-developed, have slightly shorter toes in proportion to their bodies as a whole, than the peregrine, or common falcon. The feathers of the under-parts are relatively a little larger and less dense. The moustachial streak, a narrow streak down each cheek which is a characteristic feature in most species of falcon, is narrower and less conspicuous than in the peregrine, and with age sometimes disappears altogether in certain species.

Finally, the markings on the flanks normally found in the adult bird never take the form of horizontal stripes or bars as in the peregrine. In this sub-division we may place, among the European species, the white falcon, the Iceland falcon, the gyrfalcon, the saker, the lanner, and the Alphanet lanner.

The second sub-division of long-wings is represented in Europe by a single species only: that is, the common or peregrine falcon. This falcon's tail is shorter than those of the species in the first sub-division. When folded, her wings extend almost to the tail-tip. The toes are very long, and the feathers of the under-parts are shorter and stiffer; the streaks on the plumage of the flanks in the older bird are arranged in clearly-defined horizontal bars. The moustachial stripe is much broader than in the other falcons. Although very strong, this falcon is no larger in size than the smaller species of the first sub-division.

The merlin is the sole species in the third sub-division of long-winged hawks. In some respects she resembles the sparrowhawk. This small falcon's wings are less long than is usual, covering, when folded, only the upper two-thirds of the tail. The tail itself has fewer bands than in the other falcons, and the terminal band is unusually broad. The moustachial stripe is narrow and somewhat indistinct. The beak is more compact, and the head broader and rounder than in the other long-wings. The third primary is nearly as long as the second; the first, shorter than usual, is no longer than the fourth. The merlin is the only European falcon to have the second primary emarginated on the inner web like the first, and to have a notch on the outer web of the third primary as well as on the second. The jack, after the moult, differs in his plumage from the merlin. Although small in stature, the merlin is a bold and fearless hawk, skilful and cunning in pursuit of her prey, which she likes to take by surprise as she skims low along woodland rides.

We will now proceed to the detailed descriptions of the falcons used in Europe for hawking. These are: the white falcon, the Iceland falcon, the gyrfalcon, the saker, the lanner, the Alphanet lanner, the peregrine, and the merlin.

Lanner on the fist.

42

The white falcon

A white, moulted gyrfalcon, sometimes known as a Greenland falcon, belled, jessed, and hooded, held on the falconer's fist by the leash.

Of all the hunting falcons, the white falcon is the most famous and the most sought-after. The sheer beauty of her plumage, her tractable nature, her formidable size and strength – for she is superior in this respect to all other falcons – and the difficulty of procuring a specimen, in view of the fact that the species may be found only in the vicinity of the Arctic Circle, where a trapping expedition would naturally entail vast expense – all these reasons combine to place the white falcon in the foremost rank among hunting falcons, and to make her the more prized in that the lands where she is flown are so remote from her natural haunts.

The species is easy to recognize in its adult plumage by its pale yellow beak, and the glorious white colour of the body plumage, the only colour being in the dark streakings of the upper-parts. The total length of the bird measured from the tip of the beak to the end of the tail is between 22 and 23 inches. The middle toe, not including the talon, and measured from the base of the first phalanx, may vary between $1\,5/6$ and 2 inches. The tarsus, $2\,1/3$ to $2\,1/2$ inches in length, measuring from the flat of the foot, is feathered in front for two-thirds of its length. In the female, the wings are generally $15\,1/2$ inches long and the tail $9\,1/4$ inches. The tiercel's wings are 14 to $14\,3/4$ inches long and the tail $8\,1/4$ to $8\,1/2$ inches.

In the first year, the white falcon is very similar to the juveniles of related species. The feet, the cere, and the orbits are then of a pale greenish-blue, more greyish-yellow on the soles and the scutes of the toes. The beak is dark lead-colour, tending to blackish at the tip and sometimes merging into yellowish at the base. The talons are black. The ground colour of the head, the nape, and the under-parts of the bird is white or dirty-white, with vertical streaks of dull or dark brownish or black. These streaks vary greatly in size on the different parts of the bird. They are very narrow on the throat and under wing-coverts, larger on the neck, breast, belly and leg-feathers, and very wide on the flanks, where they sometimes predominate until the ground colour itself appears as wide bars or horizontal, rounded, drop-shaped streaks. The dark colour also predominates in the centre of the neck and on the upper and hinder ear-coverts, and forms, below the corner of the mouth, an ill-defined moustachial stripe. The feathers of the top of the head have quite clearly-defined white edges, and on the brow and above the eyes white is again found in the wide eye-stripe, prolonged and broadening behind the ears towards the nape. The ground colour of the upper-parts from the neck down is dark earth-brown, verging on blackish on the remiges. All the feathers of these parts, including the secondaries, are edged with dirty-white, deepening sometimes to brownish, and are scattered, sometimes thickly, with small light spots, irregularly placed and varying in shape and size. The primary feathers, with the exception of the first three, are narrowly edged with dirty-white and have, as is usual among the falcons, wide, horizontal, light-coloured bands on the inner web, extending to two inches short of the tip of the feathers. The under wing-coverts are generally dark brown, edged with whitish; the median and greater wing-coverts have light streaks, sometimes, on the former, in the shape of round spots; while on the latter they are horizontal and arranged in bands, or bars. The tail, much darker above than below, is tipped with dirty-white and scattered throughout its length with horizontal streaks or bars of dirty yellowish-white, suffused or mottled with brown, their number varying from twelve to fourteen. The juvenile plumage of this species is, as we said earlier, greatly subject to individual variation. The streaks of the under-parts and head are sometimes narrower than the average, and in those individual birds whose dark colour is rather lighter than the normal, the tail-bands are very pronounced, the margins on the wing feathers rather wide, and the wings thickly scattered with light streaks. In other individuals, these streaks are scattered and sparse. The tail-bands, too, sometimes blend almost entirely with the ground colour; in some birds they are opposite; in others they are continuous, and their shape can vary almost endlessly.

After the first moult, the plumage of the white falcon differs considerably from the juvenile. The dark colour of the beak is now replaced by a pale yellow, except at the base and tip. The talons verge on horn-colour or yellow; but the feet, although usually yellowish in colour, often retain, after the moult, the colour of the juvenile plumage. The colour of the feathers is predominantly white, the dark colour being found only on the upper-parts; on the head and nape in the form of small, fine vertical stripes; on the back and the outer wing-coverts as heart-shaped or arrow-shaped streaks. Finally, the dark colour appears on the hinder parts of the primary feathers, leaving only a margin of varying width. However, it is by no means invariably the case, that the change in plumage produced by the moult takes place to so complete a degree as we have just described; one often finds individual birds with some dark streaks on the tail feathers; in others all the feathers of the breast and belly have little vertical or drop-shaped streaks on their centre; while the size of the streaks on the upper-parts also varies from individual to individual, so that in some birds the white colour appears only in the wide edges of the feathers, and the dark colour is sometimes arranged, on the greater wing-coverts and primaries, in more or less continuous horizontal bands, usually less clearly-marked on the anterior half of the flight-feathers.

This, of all the falconer's birds, is the best and most celebrated, thanks to the qualities it possesses in undisputed degree. It is a species used for all sorts of large game, both furred and feathered, but in particular for flying hare, kite, and heron.

In size as well as in the details of her physical structure, the Iceland falcon is very similar to the white falcon;[1] nor is it invariably an easy matter to distinguish the juveniles of the two species. Once the birds have undergone their first moult, matters are different, for it is then quite possible to distinguish the Iceland from the white falcon by the much smaller quantity of white in the plumage and by the dark beak and talons.

[1] Both white and Iceland falcons are now considered as colour-phases of the gyrfalcon.

The Iceland falcon

Haggard jerkin of the Iceland Falcon, or gyrfalcon.

46

Dessiné par M.WOLF, accessoires par C.SCHEUREN

Publié chez A.ARNZ et Comp à LEID

The description which we now give is that of the Iceland falcon in her adult plumage. At this stage, the beak is dark bluish, verging on blackish at the tip and yellow at the base. The ground colour of the head, the neck, and the under-parts from the chin to the under tail-coverts is white or whitish. All these parts, except for the chin and throat, are speckled with brown streaks, verging on slatey-blackish. These streaks form fine vertical stripes on the crown and middle ear-coverts, but are much broader on the other parts of the head and on the sides of the neck and nape; those on the crop and under tail-coverts are very long and narrow; they are small, and tear- or drop-shaped on the breast, belly, and leg-feathers, where they are lighter in hue; whilst those on the flanks are darker and broader than the others, drop- or heart-shaped, or broadening laterally so as to form horizontal streaks arranged in bars. Round the cere and near the corner of the mouth there are little, straight, black, barbless feathers, or bristles. There is no obvious moustachial stripe. The ground colour of the bird's upper-parts is blackish-brown or slate-colour, verging on reddish-grey; this colour, rather dark on the mantle, is much paler on the rump, where it verges on greyish-blue, than on the upper tail-coverts, where the dominant shade is brown; as it is also on the remiges. All the feathers of these parts are edged, widely or narrowly, with whitish, and are streaked with the same colour, but these streaks vary in shape according to their position, disappearing entirely on the lesser wing-coverts. There is usually only one light streak, not very large, and a horizontal oval in shape, on each web of the median wing-coverts and mantle; there are several more on the greater wing-coverts. On the secondaries they are broader, mottled with a darker colour, and form horizontal broken bars, whereas on the large scapulars and rump feathers they form fairly distinct bars, and the colour verges on bluish-grey. The primaries are tipped with white and have, apart from the broad light streaks usually found on the inner web, light, brown-mottled streaks arranged in bars on the outer web of the anterior half of the feathers, the streaks being neither large nor regular in shape. The outer web of the first primary is edged with white, which colour reappears towards the feather-tip as a half-dozen semicircular streaks or spots. The tail is tipped with white and has throughout its length twelve or thirteen horizontal bands of a whitish colour, as broad as the dark colour between them, and clearly stippled and splashed with brownish marbling. These bands are more clearly defined and of a purer white on the under tail-coverts, although there the ground colour is much paler than on the upper side. The greater under wing-coverts have whitish horizontal streaks arranged in bars, the other coverts having a vertical dark streak on their centre.

The Iceland falcon is in every way similar to the white falcon, both in her habits and in her temperament, and so is as highly-esteemed as that species, and used for the same varieties of game.

A belled falcon taking stand on a natural block, with its hood beside it.

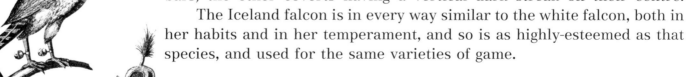

The gyrfalcon, or gerfalcon, invariably confused by naturalists with either the white or the Iceland falcon or with the saker, forms a distinct species, which up to now has only been found to breed in Norway. She resembles the white and Iceland falcons in all her physical features and in the relative proportions of the parts of the body; but she is always smaller in size, and her adult plumage is very different from that of the species we have just dealt with.[1]

The gyrfalcon

The gyrfalcon is about the same size as the tiercel white and Iceland falcons. The tiercel gyrfalcon, on the other hand, is smaller, as usual, than the female and not always even as large as the saker. He is not generally over 20 inches in length; his wings are from $12\frac{1}{2}$ to $13\frac{1}{4}$ inches long and his tail $7\frac{2}{3}$ inches. His middle toe (without the talon) is $1\frac{7}{8}$ inches; tarsus $2\frac{1}{4}$ inches; and the feathering of the front upper part of the leg extends about $1\frac{1}{4}$ inches.

In plumage, the immature gyrfalcon is very similar to the immature Iceland falcon, and shows similar individual variation. The feet at this stage are dirty olive-green, verging on yellowish, especially on the scutes of the toes. The cere and orbits are usually slightly lighter in colour than the feet in this bird.

In beauty of adult plumage, the gyrfalcon resembles the adult peregrine, except that the gyr has a few white streaks on the nape, and that her head and ear-coverts are lead-colour. The moustachial stripe is ill-defined and less dark; the streaking of the under-parts less decidedly horizontal than in the peregrine. The feet are greenish in colour, while the colouring in general varies somewhat between individuals. In structure, the gyrfalcon is quite different from the peregrine, not only in her longer tail and shorter toes, but in the other features that belong to her own sub-division. It should not be possible to confuse the two species. Compared to the Iceland falcon in the adult stage, the gyrfalcon may be distinguished, apart from her smaller size, by the almost uniform dark colouring of the ear-coverts and crown, by the more pronounced moustachial stripe, and by the dark streaks of the leg-feathers being horizontal, not vertical as in the Iceland falcon described above.

The gyrfalcon in her mature plumage has feet of a dirty olivish-green, rather paler and verging on yellow on the scutes of the toes. The cere and orbits are greenish-yellow. The beak is bluish-horn, merging into black towards the tip and into yellow at the base. The crown and sides of the head are bluish grey-black, or slate, as are the nape and sides of the neck, this colour darkening slightly towards the centre of each feather and in the moustachial stripe, which fades into the general colour of the ear-coverts, whose upper and hinder parts are slightly darker again than the front. On each side of the nape is a sort of broken collar formed of a few rows of whitish feathers, each with a broad vertical blackish streak. All the plumage of the other upper-parts of the bird, including the upper surface of the wings and their secondaries, is dark slate or slate-brown, this colour being interrupted by the black shafts of the feathers, and their bluish-grey

[1] See note on p. 46.

Left: Haggard jerkin of the gyrfalcon. Above: Haggard lanner. Below: Sore gyrfalcon.

margins and streaks. These, which run horizontally, are broader and closer-set on the greater wing-coverts and the secondaries, where they are arranged in more or less perfect bars, often mottled with brown in the centre. The light colour we have just mentioned is somewhat paler and duller on the upper tail-coverts, and predominates there, the dark colour appearing as horizontal crescent-shaped stripes. On the sides of the rump, the light colour verges on whitish, and the horizontal stripes or bars are dark grey blending into blue-violet. The ground colour of the remiges darkens to blackish-brown; the brownish-grey streaks on their outer webs fade towards the end of the feathers, which have a narrow white edge, the streaks on the inner web, however, being quite pale on the underside of the wings, whilst on the upper side they are more reddish-brown; this again changing to white on the anterior feathers. The light-coloured tail-bands, fourteen or fifteen in number, are dirtier in colour than the streaks of the upper-parts, and have, especially towards the centre, a mottling of light brown. The tail-bands are quite broad, the dark colour appearing in the form of narrow bands, sometimes opposite, sometimes continuous, sometimes bow- or crescent-shaped, and darker towards the tip of the tail, which is whitish or dirty-white. The underside of the tail is as usual much paler in colour than the upper side. The lesser under wing-coverts have dark vertical streaks; the medians have light streaks, sometimes round or oval in shape; these are horizontal on the greater coverts. The ground colour of the underparts is fairly pure white with streaks of dark slate colour, verging on brown. These streaks, in the form of fine vertical stripes on the chin and throat, become more h-shaped on the front of the neck and the crop, the h being evenly wide. On the breast and belly, the streaks are very narrow at the base, but grow wider towards the ends of the feathers to appear there tear-shaped or drop-shaped; they are rather dark on the flanks, where the upper ones are heart-shaped, the lower ones lozenge-shaped and more or less exactly like those of the horizontal bands. Horizontal streaks in the form of close-set bars, not so dark in colour, are also found on the leg-feathers. The streaks on the under tail-coverts are small, sparse, and lozenge-shaped, and are prolonged in fine dark stripes down the shafts of the feathers.

In captivity, the gyrfalcon is usually found to be decidedly different in temperament from the white and Iceland falcons; she is contrary and obstinate; cantankerous, and sometimes vicious to the extent of attacking other falcons, of whatever species; and when flying in a cast she may crab, or stoop at her companion instead of the quarry. The gyrfalcon is used for the same kinds of hawking as the other two large northern falcons; but the tiercel is too small and hence too weak to be flown at hare or rabbit.

The saker

The saker, or sacre, used in falconry is a bird slightly larger than the lanner falcon, so that as far as size is concerned she may be ranked between that species and the gyrfalcon. Her plumage may be distinguished from that of the two latter by a greater variation in colour in the juvenile, and by the lack of light-coloured bands on the deck feathers of the tail. In her adult dress she differs from all other adult falcons by her duller colouring, similar to that of juvenile birds, and by the lack of transverse streaks on both upper and underparts.

The saker's wings are 14 1/2 inches long; those of the sakret only 13 1/2 inches. The saker's tail is 8 3/4 inches long; the sakret's, 8 inches. The middle toe in the saker is between 1 7/8 and 2 inches; in the sakret 1 2/3 inches. The tarsus is feathered on its upper front section for half its length. The tail exceeds the folded wings in length by 1 1/4 or 1 1/2 inches.

Individual birds in their first year, though similar, generally speaking, to the juven ile gyrfalcon in plumage, differ from the latter in the following particulars. The ground colour of the upper-parts is less dark, particularly on the tail, and inclines more to brown. There are only a few isolated light streaks on the large scapulars, these streaks, like the edges of the feathers, being pale brown-red or rust-colour, lighter on the edges of the primaries. There is more white on the nape and back of the head, and here too are found tinges of a very pale brown-red. The tip of the tail is white-edged; light streaks are usually only found on the inner webs of the five lateral pairs of tail-feathers; these number ten or eleven and are broader than they are long, sometimes even oval, or nearly round, in shape. The streakings of the under-parts, usually a very dark brown, are generally a little narrower than in the young gyrfalcon, often no more than a fine, dark stripe running along the shafts of the under tail-coverts. The ear-patch always has, in the centre, a white mark; and white predominates on the forehead and eye-stripe. The remiges are streaked on their inner webs only with the lighter colour. The feet, cere, and orbits, are dull greenish-blue, changing to yellowish on the scutes of the toes.

After the moult, the plumage of the saker undergoes the following changes. The ground colour of the upper-parts is paler, particularly on the tail; the margins of the feathers are broader – rich rufous on the feathers of the back and wings, considerably paler on the tail-feathers and secondaries. The feathers of the crown also have a fairly broad edging of pale rust-brown fading to white. The moustachial stripe, broken by a few whitish feathers, is poorly marked. The chin, throat, and under tail-coverts are a uniform dirty-white, and this is the predominant colour of the other under-parts, the streaks here being smaller and less dark in colour than in the juvenile. These streaks are drop-shaped, rather small on the breast, belly, and leg-feathers, much broader on the flanks. Those on the lesser and median under wing-coverts are vertical; but the white streaks of the greater coverts are horizontal and arranged in bars. The talons, as in the immature bird, are uniformly black, and the beak bluish horn, changing to black towards the tip and to yellow at the base. The feet, together with the cere and the orbits, are more distinctly yellowish than in the young birds.

The saker is used for the same kinds of hawking as the peregrine, and she may even be flown at kite; but the sakret is not strong enough for such quarry. The bird is only occasionally obtained by falconers, however, as it is found only in eastern Europe and western Asia.

The lanner

The bird we here introduce under the name of the lanner falcon, has ever been considered the most beautiful of the birds used in falconry, owing to the pleasing colours of her plumage. Not so large as the saker, she is equal in size to the peregrine, but may be distinguished from the latter by those characteristics proper to the group to which she belongs, as well as by a marked difference in colour.

In the tiercel, or lanneret, the wings are about $12\,1/4$ inches long; the tail $6\,7/8$ inches; and the middle toe $1\,2/3$ inches. The lanner's wings are $12\,3/4$ inches long; tail $7\,7/8$ inches, and middle toe $1\,3/4$ inches. In the length of the tarsi and the extent of the leg feathering, the species is very similar to the peregrine, but this is not true of the feet, cere, and eye-orbits, which are more similar in colour to those of the saker.

The plumage of the juvenile lanner is very like that of the juvenile saker, but with the following differences. The markings on the plumage of the crown are narrower, the dominant colour in that region being the whitish colour of the edges of the feathers. The rufous tint of the back of the head and nape is slightly less vivid. The light edges to the feathers of the upper-parts are less distinct, and their colour shades more into rust-colour than in the saker; these parts are mottled with very pale russet-brown spots, distributed irregularly here and there, their shape and size varying a good deal with the individual bird. The ground colour of the tail is a little darker than in the saker; but is broken, on both the outer and the inner webs of the tail-feathers, by light horizontal streaks running in bars. The number of these broken bars may be eleven or twelve, their colour being precisely the colour of the streaks on the wings. The streaks on the bird's under-parts are generally narrower than in the saker. The lesser under wing-coverts have dark, vertical streaks; the medians are spotted with whitish marks, usually round in shape; and the greater wing-coverts bear light, transverse streaks running in bands.

In her adult plumage, the lanner is similar in colour both to the adult peregrine and the adult gyrfalcon, but may be distinguished from both at a glance by the beautiful reddish colour of the nape and crown, as well as by a number of other characteristic features. The forehead and lores are whitish at this age. The feathers of the other parts of the crown, and those of the nape, are pale brown-rust, with blackish-brown vertical streaks down the middle. These streaks are very broad on the feathers of the centre of the nape, the dark colour there appearing more in the shape of a large spot. The moustachial stripe is narrow but quite well-defined. The ear-coverts are whitish, verging decidedly on reddish-yellow, with dark vertical streaks, predominating and more or less effacing the ground colour in the upper and hinder parts of the ear-patches. The orbits are surrounded with black feathers, and an indistinct stripe of the same colour runs from the eyes behind the ears and down the sides of the nape. The ground colour of the other upper-parts is blackish-brown or slate. All the feathers of these parts, as well as the secondaries, bear light transverse streaks, arranged in bars on the scapulars, the greater wing-coverts, and the secondaries, and also on the rump, but disappearing entirely on the lesser wing-coverts. This light colour is a bluish-grey, fairly bright on the lower back and rump, dirtier and mottled with brownish on the other parts, and verging on brown-rust towards the leading edge of the wing-tip. The primaries are, apart from lighter streaks on the inner webs, blackish-brown with whitish edgings. The ground colour of the tail is paler than that of the wings, and is broken by a dozen horitontal bands of moderate breadth, coloured dirty-white suffused with grey-brown, the tail-tip being whitish. The lesser under wing-coverts have dark vertical streaks; the medians have whitish spots, round and fairly regular; whilst on the greater wing-coverts the streaks are horizontal and run in bands. The predominant colour of the under-parts is white shading to a quite bright, pale, reddish-yellow. The chin, the throat, and sometimes the feathers of the crop, are of a uniform whitish; whilst the other under-parts have blackish-brown streaks. These streaks are heart-shaped on the breast and belly; on the flank-feathers they are much larger and arranged in wide, irregular, horizontal bands; those on the leg-feathers being also horizontal but less dark in colour; whereas on the under tail-coverts these dark streaks are usually vertical and quite narrow.

The Alphanet or Tunisian lanner

These are the names given by falconers of an earlier period to a bird differing from the common lanner only by some variation in colour. This variation, although slight, is, as far as we can establish, constant; and as the bird does not appear to inhabit those countries frequented by the lanner, we have thought it proper to follow the example of earlier writers on falconry and treat the Alphanet lanner separately by introducing her as a subspecies of the true lanner.

The Alphanet lanner resembles the common lanner at all points, in size, and in the relative proportions of tail, wings, and feet, as well as in the colour of the cere, the orbits, and the feet. It seems that this subspecies varies as much in size as does the peregrine.

In her first year, the Alphanet lanner differs not at all from the juvenile lanner, but once she has assumed her adult plumage, her colouring differs from that of the adult lanner in the following ways. The dark streaks of the back of the head and nape are much narrower and often cover only the shafts of the feathers, thus allowing the reddish colour of those areas to predominate. This colour verges on bright brown-rust, the head-plumage recalling to some extent the shrike, *Lanius rufus.*[1] The forehead, except on its anterior part, tends to blackish-brown, and this colour

[1]Sic Schlegel & v. Wulverhorst. I cannot, however, trace *L. rufus* in modern bird handbooks. The shrike whose colouring most nearly conforms to that of the lanner described is the Woodchat Shrike, *L. senator,* whose head and nape are bright chestnut and whose forehead and ear-coverts are blackish. The more common Red-backed Shrike, *L. collurio,* does not fit the bill, for the male has a grey crown and nape and the female is duller brown. The name of Rufous Shrike was formerly given to the Rufous Vanga, a somewhat similar species, but unlikely to be the bird referred to as it is confined to Madagascar.

runs above the eyes and along the sides of the head, as well as down the upper and hinder ear-patches, and is then prolonged downwards into the moustachial stripe, which is darker, as well as broader, than in the lanner. The ground colour of the back, the back of the neck, and the upper side of the wings, is more brown, and the light edgings and streaks of the feathers in these parts is less pronounced, often fading more or less entirely into the ground colour. The rump has dirtier colouring, and the light tail-bands are much less clearly-marked than in the lanner. The under-parts of the bird from the crop down have a decided tint of pale rust-brown, which may also be found on the under wing-coverts. The leg-feathers are often vertically streaked.

Following pages: Left: Sore tiercel peregrine falcon, very young, said to be in Kestrel's plumage.

Right: Haggard peregrine falcon.

The falcon[1]

This species is not generally given a special name by falconers, as it is the most widely-distributed of all falcons and, at least in Europe, the falcon normally used in hawking. In referring to the bird merely as the common or ordinary falcon, we are following the example set by Dutch, English, German, and Danish falconers, all of whom, when comparing the bird to other species in the genus, do likewise.

The common falcon, then, differs in several respects from the other large European species; her toes being longer, her feathers, particularly on the under-parts, being in general smaller, her tail being proportionately shorter, hardly protruding beyond the wings when the latter are closed. There is the further difference compared with the other species we have described, that the moustachial stripe is broader and more conspicuous, and that in the juvenile the plumage of the under-parts is more closely streaked, while the markings of the flanks and legs in the mature bird are more clearly arranged in horizontal bars.

The common European falcons are subject to considerable variation in size. The total length of the tiercel varies between 14 and 15 inches; his wings are between 11 and 12 inches; his tail between $5\frac{1}{2}$ and $5\frac{3}{4}$ inches, and his middle toe about $1\frac{3}{4}$ inches long. The peregrine's length is between 16 and 18 inches; her wings between $12\frac{3}{4}$ and $13\frac{1}{2}$ inches; her tail between 6 and $6\frac{1}{2}$ inches, and her middle toe between 2 and $2\frac{1}{8}$ inches. The talons in both immature and mature birds are dead black, but the colour of the feet varies a good deal in this species according to age and according to the individual bird.

The plumage of the immature falcon is in general similar in colour to that of the young saker, except that the moustachial stripe is much more pronounced; there is less white on the nape, and no trace of the rufous tint; the markings of the under-parts are smaller and closer-set, the falcon's feathers being smaller than those of the saker; and the outer webs of the tail-feathers have light streaks, as do the inner webs. The feet, the

[1] The common falcon is now always referred to in English as the peregrine (or tiercel, if male), and this word will be used in later pages of the book, rather than 'common falcon', which the French has.

57

Dessiné par M. WOLF, accessoires par SCHEUREN.   Publié chez A. ARNZ et Comp. à LEID

cere, and the orbits of the eyes are pale bluish-green, and thus very light; but this colour also is highly variable, rarely appearing exactly the same in any two individuals. The beak, as is usual in falcons, is dirty dark-blue, verging on blackish towards the tip and changing to yellow at the base. The ground colour of the upper-parts is a dull, rather dark, brown, slightly lighter on the tail and deepening to blackish on the remiges; the same colour appears on the upper and hinder ear-coverts, and delineates, forward of this region, a moustachial stripe much broader than in the other large European falcons. The feathers of the upper-parts are edged with rust-brown, and those of the wings, the back, and the rump are often stippled here and there with little, very light, dirty rust-brown spots, whose number and shape are no less variable according to the individual than the shadings of the ground colour. The tail-feathers, tipped with white, have on both webs ten or eleven light, horizontal streaks, similar in colour to the light streaks on the wings, and running in bands. As usual, the inner webs of the remiges have light, rather wide, transverse streaks, close-scattered. The under wing-coverts are dark brown; the lesser ones have a fairly wide whitish margin; the medians have whitish, usually oval-shaped streaks; the greater have narrower streaks running in bands. The predominant colour of the under-parts is dirty white, verging to various shades of pale rust-brown, especially on the breast, the belly, and the flanks. The feathers of these parts are, from the throat down, marked with a dark brown vertical streak; these streaks are usually quite broad, particularly on the flanks; those on the under tail-coverts being, however, transversely placed. The white of the underparts extends as far as the middle of the ear-patch; it appears on each side of the neck in scattered, irregular, indistinct streaks; and more streaks of white may be seen on the nape, where they coalesce in the shape of a poorly-marked semi-collar. The forehead of this bird is also a whitish colour.

The plumage acquired after the first moult is very different from that of the juvenile falcon. The feet, the cere, and the orbits are now a fairly bright yellow. Only very little white remains on the forehead, whilst the white streaks on the nape disappear completely. The ground colour of the upper-parts changes to a brownish-black. All the feathers of these parts, from the neck down, are, like the secondaries, edged and streaked quite clearly with ashy-grey verging on bluish; these streaks, however, are not found on the lesser wing-coverts. Further back they are broader, coalescing to form bars; on the rump they become predominant, the ground colour appearing only as narrow, horizontal bars. The light tail-bands, similar in colour to the barrings of the other upper-parts, are twelve or thirteen in number on the upper surface of the tail, and are set close, especially towards the base of the tail, where the ground colour appears as very narrow bands. The tail-tip is white, and the terminal tail-band is black and rather broader than the others. The under tail-coverts are as usual much paler in hue than the upper. The ground colour of the upper-parts of the bird is white or dirty-white, often suffused with yellowish-rust, especially on the breast and belly. All the under-parts, from the throat down, are streaked with black verging on reddish-brown; the streaks, fairly narrow and vertical on the crop, are heart-shaped or rounded on the breast, the belly, and the upper feathers of the flanks; on the lower part of the belly they are horizontal, and on the under tail-coverts they run in horizontal bars, as they do also on the leg-feathers and the large flank feathers, where they are rather broad. The white of the under-parts extends usually more or less distinctly up into the ear-patch, so that the conspicuous moustachial stripe is quite clearly differentiated from the dark colour of the head; it sometimes happens, however, that the ear-coverts are uniformly black, in which case the moustachial stripe blends completely with this colour. The streakings of the under wing-coverts run fairly decidedly in a horizontal direction. The wide whitish streaks on the outer webs of the remiges verge towards the front of the wings on reddish-brown.

The succeeding moults (that is, those which take place after the bird has reached the second year of age) do not bring about such decided changes in the colours of the plumage as does the first. The ground colour of the upper-parts is, however, darker, and the light streaks or bars on these parts become brighter in colour, as do the edges of the feathers, so that they contrast more clearly with the ground colour. The streaks on the under-parts are smaller, the horizontal bars narrower, and the light colour of the flank feathers and leg feathers verges more on bluish-grey.

Among the juvenile birds of this species there may be observed a group with rather different plumage. In these birds, the light colour is pale, dirty rust-brown, verging on yellowish on the sides of the neck. The feathers of the upper-parts have broad margins of the same colour. The orbits and the cere are dirty greyish-blue verging very faintly on greenish; the beak is a darker blue changing to blackish at the tip. The feet are very pale dirty yellow. This colour-phase is known to falconers as the 'kestrel-feathered falcon'. According to them, these birds are more difficult to train than the others, so much so that in many cases nothing can be made of them at all; but on the other hand, one may be found now and again which seems peculiarly amenable to training, and such an individual can be made into an excellent hawk. But some falconers maintain that these young birds assume, after the first moult, an adult plumage similar to that of the usual adult birds. The most noteworthy colour-phase among adults is one with very dark upper-parts, the black of the sides of the head blending into the moustachial stripe and extending over the greather part of the ear-coverts. The other variants that may be met with amongst adult falcons usually display only slight differences in the shades of the colours, and in the shape and size of the streakings on the under-parts.

The common falcon has been observed in most European countries with the exception of Iceland. The place selected for building the eyrie is usually a cranny high up a cliff, but tall trees such as pine and fir are occasionally chosen. The eyrie is crudely built of twigs put together without apparent art, as is generally the case among birds of prey. The clutch usually consists of three eggs, rather round in shape, of a yellowish-grey or reddish-yellow colour and freckled with brown or reddish-brown. The

Following pages: Left: Haggard merlin, her jack (above), and a sore merlin.

Right: Haggard goshawk.

61

Dessiné par M. WOLF, accessoires par O. SAAL.   Publié chez A. ARNZ et Comp. à LEIDE.

nestlings hatch out after three weeks, and frequently leave the nest before they are fully-fledged. At this season of the year, the birds resort to forests and woodlands, perching at night in the trees. As winter approaches, they usually leave their customary haunts and either come down to the lowlands, where they take up residence in any district offering them the prospect of adequate food; or else emigrate abroad, if the summer was spent in cooler countries. In Europe, birds of passage are found in autumn, and even sometimes throughout the winter, in those open plains stretching along the northern coasts of Germany and the Low Countries; and can also be found there in the spring, during the return migration to their summer quarters. It appears that these migrations are governed by definite laws; for our falconers have often observed that, in the autumn, the first birds to arrive are the adults of both sexes, followed first by the young tiercels, and lastly by the young peregrines; whereas in the spring, the number of passage hawks in these districts is much smaller and almost entirely confined to young peregrines, the birds taken only occasionally turning out to be either young tiercels or adult falcons. We must suppose that the regular nature of their migrations is subject to such circumstances as the abundance or scarcity of game in different districts, the weather, and above all, the wind. This falcon will eat all kinds of medium-sized game, such as duck, pheasant, partridge, pigeon, curlew, woodcock, etc. Smaller birds such as snipe, thrushes, larks, etc. may also be taken, and even, in the absence of anything better, crows, jackdaws, jays, and gulls. Pigeon is eagerly hunted, and in winter the peregrine will often take up residence in the middle of towns or villages, pitching on towers or other high buildings, in order to find this favourite food of hers, spreading terror daily among the local pigeon population until she is killed.

Having caught her prey, the peregrine then carries it off to some point in the fields where she will eat it; but it often happens that, if she sees a buzzard or kite approaching, she will abandon her prey to these cowardly birds – a curious fact, which can only be explained by supposing that the peregrine fears low-flying aggressors, since she is ill-equipped to ward off attack from the ground.

The peregrine is the bird most commonly used for hawking in Europe, not only because of her fine flying qualities, but because she is, of course, much easier to procure than the other large falcons, She may be trained to fly all kinds of quarry, such as, for example, crows, magpies, partridge, duck, etc. She is not really suitable for flying at kite, and for flights at heron the passage peregrine should be used, never the tiercel. Eyass peregrines wait on well for flights at partridge, duck, crows, magpies, and other medium-sized birds.

The merlin

The merlin is the smallest of the hawks. She may be distinguished from the other noble falcons of Europe, as from the other birds in the genus, by a large number of characteristics which to some extent are common to the sparrowhawks.

The male, or jack, merlin, is approximately 11 inches long; the merlin 12 inches. The wings of the jack are 8 inches long; of the merlin, 8 1/2 inches. The jack's tail is 4 3/4 inches; the merlin's 5 1/4 inches. The wings, when closed, extend at their tip only about as far as two-thirds of the length of the tail. The second primary is scarcely longer than the third, and has, like the first, a deep notch on the inner web. The third primary has a slight notch on the outer web, as has the first. The first and fourth primaries are equal in length. The head is broader and rounder than in the other long-wings, and the beak more compact. The feet are well-developed, and yellow in colour, as are the cere and the eye-orbits.

The juvenile merlin has dark brown upper-parts with a greyish gloss, verging on blackish on the primaries. All the feathers of these parts are edged with pale reddish-brown, the shafts being marked with a blackish stripe. The feathers of the back and wings also have horizontal streaks, those on the large wing-feathers being brighter in hue than the rest. The tail has six narrow bands of a whitish brown-rust, and the tail-tip is edged in white. The bird's under-parts, from the neck down, are dirty-white verging sometimes on brownish, but all the feathers of these parts bear broad vertical streaks of a dull brown-rust, the streaks being narrower and paler on the leg feathers and the under tail-coverts. The throat is pure white; and white is also found on the forehead and ear-coverts. The eye-stripe is conspicuous and of a brownish-white; it generally runs down as far as the nape, which has a whitish semi-collar, the white broken by the dark streakings of the feathers. The merlin in her adult plumage is exactly similar to the juvenile, except in the colour of her upper-parts, which is slatey, and of the lighter tail-bands, which is pale whitish-grey suffused with brownish and mottled with blackish-grey. The cere and orbits are often pale bluish. The jack differs considerably from the juveniles and the merlin after the first moult, when the plumage of his upper-parts is slatey dark grey verging on bluish. The black stripes along the shafts of the feathers are clearly marked. The light bars of the primaries are whitish and the under wing-coverts spotted with white, these spots usually round in shape. The tip of the tail is white, and there is a very broad terminal tail-band, black in colour, and seven narrower ones, often blending into the upper part of the tail. The chin and throat are whitish; the feathers of the forehead and eye-stripe, like the ear-coverts, are white verging on brown-rust and marked with narrow blackish vertical stripes. The moustachial stripe is very poorly marked. The under tail-coverts are greyish-white verging on brown and are striped vertically with blackish-brown, narrow stripes. The collar and all the under-parts from the throat to the vent are yellowish brown-rust, and have dark brown vertical streaks, narrow on the leg feathers, broader elsewhere, especially on the flanks, where they are often horizontal. These streaks become much narrower after the second moult, at which stage the under-parts are brighter and cleaner in colour.

The merlin, alone among the smaller European falcons, is esteemed as a hunting bird, although the tiercel is never used for this purpose. As she has a gentle and confiding disposition she may quite often be made in a

very short time, and may not even need to be made to the hood. She is used for flights at all kinds of small birds, but her especial quarry has always been the lark. In former days the merlin was also used to encourage falcons being flown at heron to mount up well, both merlin and falcons being cast off simultaneously.

European falcons not used for hawking

Apart from the long-winged hawks we have just described, the continent of Europe supports five other species of falcon which are not suitable, or only barely suitable, for hawking; but which we now propose to mention briefly, partly because they are referred to in most books on falconry, and partly because we should be able to distinguish them from other hawks of the lure mentioned above.

Two of these species, the hobby and the sapphire falcon, although noble falcons by virtue of their physical characteristics, form a small sub-division in the class, distinguished by the length of the wings, which when closed are as long as or longer than the tip of the tail.[1] These birds are smaller than the other European falcons, apart from the merlin, that is. Like the merlin, their heads are rounded and broad, and their upper-parts, in the mature plumage, uniformly dark in colour. Not being aggressive by nature, and not possessing the skill, when reared in captivity, to seize the quarry in their feet with the necessary ease, they are unsuited to the chase. The other three species are the kestrel, the lesser kestrel, and the red-footed falcon. These birds form the group of ignoble falcons. Their toes are short, and the tubercles not prominent, and being for this reason incapable of seizing birds on the wing, they are of no use for hunting. These ignoble falcons fall into two lesser sub-divisions, one including the red-footed falcon, and the other the kestrels. The wings of the red-footed falcon are as long as the tail, which in the mature bird has no tail-bands; the first primary, the only one with a notch on the inner web, is at least as long as the third; and the colouring of the plumage is very different from that of the other falcons. The kestrels have looser plumage; their wings do not extend to the tip of the tail, which is rather long and somewhat fan-shaped; in general, only the first primary is notched on the inner web. This feather is not quite as long as the fourth, whereas the third is almost the same length as the second. In flight, these birds have a habit of hovering[2] in the air whilst scanning the ground for their prey, fanning their wings and spreading their tail, and sometimes remaining thus for a considerable time, which helps to distinguish them from other birds of prey.

Sore tiercel goshawk.

[1] The sapphire falcon is probably Eleonora's Falcon, *F. Eleonorae.*
[2] Hence their familiar names of *windhover,* and *hoverhawk.*

67

The short-winged hawks

The birds known in Europe as the short-winged hawks are the goshawk and the sparrowhawk. These birds, very different from one another as far as mere size is concerned, are nevertheless related in all other essential characteristics, in consequence of which they have been placed by naturalists in the same family of accipiters, or hawks. They differ from the long-wings in a number of ways, chief among which are the short, rounded wings, the absence of a tooth on the upper mandible, the longer tarsi, covered back and front with broad scales, the iris of the eye, which is always a rather deep yellow, the lack of a membrane or orbit round the eye; and in several other, less obvious ways, including their habits and ways of life.

The wings of the short-winged hawks, when closed, scarcely cover more than the upper half of the tail. The large flight-feathers have different proportions from the corresponding feathers in the falcons. In the goshawk and sparrowhawk, the longest primary is not the second, but the fourth; the third is somewhere between the fifth and sixth in length, the second somewhere between the sixth and seventh; and the tip of the first primary hardly reaches as far as the tip of the ninth. The first five primaries are all emarginated on the inner web from a point halfway down right to the tip, and there is an obvious notch on the outer webs of the second and all succeeding primaries up to the sixth. The tarsi of hawks of the first are longer than those of the falcons, and only feathered on their upper portions, at the front and sides, near the tarsal joint; their reticulation is wider and more regular, broadening fore and aft into large scutes. The toes are quite long, especially in the sparrowhawk, and are furnished beneath with tubercles, as in the falcons. Their heads are smaller than the heads of the falcons, and more flattened on the top. Their beaks, strongly curved, are rather compact and have a single festoon on the edge of the upper mandible, very obvious, but rounded, and not so near the tip as the tooth of the falcons; the edges of the lower mandible have no obvious notch. The eyes are smaller, the iris always a glowing yellow, and there is no naked skin round them as there is in the falcons. They have long tails with a small number of rather broad, dark, tail-bands. The nares, or nostrils, are slanted and oval. The feathers are usually blunter in shape, especially on the scapulars, whereas those of the nape and crown are more pointed. Those forming the dark parts of the plumage are always whitish in colour from the base to about the middle.

The hawks of the fist are cunning, brave, and bold to the highest degree, and more savage in temperament than all the other birds of prey put together. In this respect they might be compared to the tiger, whilst the temperament of the falcons is more analogous to the lion. They do not fly as fast, nor as long, as the falcons, but they are agile and quick on the turn, which enables them to hunt in woods and plantations, to pursue their prey right into cover and truss to it either on the wing or on foot, or when sitting or crouching. They have a habit of flying low, so as to take their prey by surprise. Their prey consists of small or medium-sized birds and mammals. They generally build high up in the branches.

The goshawk may be recognized at a glance by the shortness of her wings, which, alone among the larger European birds of prey, are so short that they cover only half the tail when closed. The goshawk's total length is about 22 inches, but the tiercel is usually no more than 19 inches long. The goshawk's wings are 13½ inches long, tail 10 inches, tarsus 3⅜ inches, and middle toe 2 inches. The tiercel's wings are 12½ inches long, tail 9 inches, tarsus 3 inches, and middle toe 1⅔ inches. From this it will be noted that the goshawk is the equal of the larger falcons in size, even though her wings are shorter. Her toes are as long as the falcons' toes, and equally strong, if not stronger, though the tubercles on their under-sides are less prominent.

The goshawk

The goshawk's eyes are a glowing yellow, in the adult birds deepening to orange-yellow; the cere and feet are also yellow, paler in the juveniles, brighter in the adults. The beak is blackish-blue. The pounces are black and strongly curved; that on the outer toe is small, those on the inner and middle toes are very large. Between the outer and middle toes is a web or sheath, uniting these toes at their base. The tail, slightly rounded at the tip, has five or six dark tail-bands.

The ground colour of the goshawk's under-parts is, in the juvenile birds, whitish shading to yellowish-rust or pale rusty-brown, except on the throat. All the feathers of these parts have dark brown vertical streaks, very narrow on the throat, somewhat wider on the other parts, especially the flanks, and running to a point at the tips of the feathers. The ground colour of the upper-parts is fairly dark brown, but always lighter on the head and neck, where the feathers are edged with light yellowish-brown. The rump feathers are similar. The feathers of the other upper-parts usually have a paler margin. The primaries are blackish-brown, broken by whitish or greyish mottled bars; there are similar bars on the rump. The dark tail-bands are clearly marked, and distinctly separated by similar bands of pale yellowish-brown, stippled or spotted with blackish-brown. Finally, the plumage of the juvenile goshawk, although similar in both male and female, shows a high level of variation between individual birds, though without altering the general arrangement of colours to any great extent. After the moult, when the goshawk assumes her mature plumage, somewhere towards the end of her second summer, her colouring is quite different from that of the juvenile. The upper-parts are now sooty blackish-brown shading more or less into bluish-grey. There is a conspicuous white eye-stripe, prolonged down the back of the head to the nape, the white feathers that form it having dark streaks at their tips. The ground colour of the under-parts is more or less pure white; all the feathers of these parts have brown-black shafts and (except on the throat and under tail-coverts) wavy horizontal stripes, quite close-set, and also brown-black in colour. The tail tip is edged in white, its blackish bands often merging with the ground colour along their edges. The adult tiercel differs from the mature goshawk only in his smaller size, the narrower and closer dark bars, the purer white of the under-parts, the darker colour of the head, and the beautiful dark ashy-bluish tint of the mantle and upper-parts, which

colour disappears more or less completely after death, giving way to a smoky brown-grey.

The favourite haunts of the goshawk are woods and forests. Although a migratory bird, a small number of goshawks will usually be found over-wintering as visitors in their summer quarters, not, as then, settling in any fixed locality, but moving from place to place seeking for food. The goshawk feeds on all kinds of creatures, medium-sized and small. She is one of the worst enemies of the pigeon tribe; she will also take leveret and rabbit, and if there is nothing more to her taste she will even deign to eat voles. Her eyrie is built in the tallest forest and woodland trees. The clutch is three or four greenish-white eggs, usually scattered with yellowish-brown speckles. The young hatch out after three weeks.

The goshawk, held in low esteem by true amateurs and writers on falconry, for reasons which will become clear when we turn to game-hawking, has been better appreciated among those whose limited means or other circumstances prevent them from owning falcons. The goshawk is used principally for flights at partridge, pheasant, and rabbit; formerly she was also flown at waterfowl. The training of the goshawk presents fewer difficulties than the training of the large falcons. To fly a goshawk, it is not necessary to own more than one bird. In former times, goshawks were kept in the kitchens, and it was for this reason, and because hunting with her always meant some sort of addition to the game-larder, that she was known in days gone by as 'the cook's hawk'.

The sparrowhawk

The sparrowhawk is akin to the goshawk in the details of her physical structure as well as in her appearance; her wings are, relatively, as short as the goshawk's, and her tail as long; the primaries follow roughly the same proportions of length and bear the same number of notches; but she is only half the size of the goshawk, her tarsi are more slender and somewhat longer, and her toes longer, thinner, and with more prominent tubercles, and are thus less powerful.

The sparrowhawk's total length is between $11\frac{1}{2}$ and 14 inches. In the male, or musket, the wings are $7\frac{3}{4}$ inches long, the tarsus $2\frac{1}{2}$ inches, the tail $5\frac{1}{2}$ inches, and the middle toe $1\frac{1}{3}$ inches. The female, or spar, has wings $6\frac{3}{4}$ inches long, middle toe $1\frac{1}{2}$ inches, tail $6\frac{3}{4}$ inches, and tarsus $2\frac{1}{4}$ inches. The sparrowhawk's pounces are strongly curved, very sharp, and black in colour. The beak is sharply hooked and pointed, and is blackish-blue. The iris and the feet are pure yellow, very bright in the adult bird. The tail, slightly rounded at the tip, and edged with white, has five or six dark bands; the wing feathers all bear a broad, light streak, which shows only when the feathers are ruffled. The sparrowhawk's plumage differs considerably according to age and, in the mature bird, to sex. In the juvenile, the ground colour of the malar region and the upper-parts is fairly dark brown; all the feathers of these parts are edged in pale, dirty brown-rust; the remiges are dark brown, broken by broad, blackish

Sore sparrowhawk and haggard musket. The landscape includes the village of Valkenswaard.

African Crowned Hawk-Eagle. A very powerful bird that takes monkeys and small buck in the wild. Not a very good falconry bird owing to its size and weight.

horizontal bars, the edges of the inner webs being white. The under-parts of the bird and the eye-stripe are whitish with some dark brown streaks, vertical on the throat, the sides of the neck and the eye-stripe, heart- or arrow-shaped on the crop, and arranged in wavy horizontal stripes on the breast, belly, leg feathers, and under tail-coverts. The young musket differs from the spar of the year only in having a warmer tinge to his dark colours, the streaks on the feathers of the crop being broader, and heart-shaped rather than arrow-shaped. After the first moult, the spar has upper-parts of dark brownish-grey, shading slightly to bluish. The ground colour of the under-parts is cleaner than in the juveniles; the stripes here are narrower, and those on the crop are more decidedly horizontal. After the second moult, these stripes become narrower still, and the ground colour of the upper-parts is a more distinct bluish. The musket, after the first moult, differs from the mature female in the cleaner grey-blue of his upper-parts, and in the brighter russet of the streaks on the under-parts, which colour is also to be found on the back malar region, the sides of the neck, the flanks, and the feathers of the back of the leg.

The sparrowhawk likes to take smaller birds, such as thrushes, partridge chicks, quail, titmice, bunting, and especially finches and sparrows; she will also take voles, and even insects. Flying low along the ground, she is adept at taking her prey by surprise; her daring and agility on the turn enable her to seize her prey with equal ease whether on the wing, perched in a tree, or crouching on the ground; the pursuit often takes her right into cover, sometimes even into farmyards, stables or houses. The musket, however, is not as courageous, nor as strong, as the spar.

pour le chaulme qui y eft court
et les pinçons fi affient bolen
tiers Et foit tendue amfi côme
bous bees en la pourtraiture Et
es · iiij · cachettes doit auoir · pi
çons pour appeller les paffans

Et en la meute ceft la berife
fourtrace qui eft en my la tir
doit auoir · ij · pinçons qui tien
dront par les piez ou p̄ne
efle Et amfi tendres pour la
fondre des pinçons apres la

the methods of taking, managing, and training hawks

Hawks may be procured either by taking them from the eyrie as eyasses, or by setting traps for them when fully-grown.[1] When taking eyasses from the wild, it is better to choose the period when they are still partly covered in down, with their contour feathers only about an inch long. If the birds are to be transported long distances, they must be placed in a basket with straw in the bottom. If the birds belong to the species that commonly nest in trees, such as the goshawk, sparrowhawk, and saker, it is easy to take the young birds from the nest; but with the other large falcons, whose eyries are normally built on precipitous cliffs, the enterprise is often fraught with danger. He who wishes to emerge from it with a whole skin must not be a faintheart.

There is a variety of ways of taking fully-grown birds, according to the species it is desired to obtain, or rather according to that species' field-character and habits.

The different species of large falcons may be captured in different ways. The most common method of taking all kinds of birds of prey, but especially peregrines, and certainly the method which holds out the greatest hope of success, can be used only in certain localities and with the aid of rather complicated devices, and it further demands a great deal of experience, so if success is to be ensured, it is absolutely necessary to be guided by an expert in the field, or by a professional falconer. The most favourable terrain for this kind of trapping is that immense plain extending all along the northern part of Germany, through Holland and across the Atlantic coasts of France, right down to the borders of Spain. Along this route, in the autumn of each year, the birds of passage which have summered in colder regions wend their way back southwards across the open plains to settle for the winter wherever good foraging may be found. To these wide heaths, at the autumn migration, go the falconers, to spread

---

[1] All wild birds being protected in Gt. Britain, it is illegal to kill, take, or cage a wild bird except under licence.

Page left: An illustration from *Le Livre du Roy Modus et de la Royne Ratio* shows a method of trapping falcons to be trained for falconry by means of nets and decoys.

their nets for the hawks, confident of attracting to them all the hawks that are sojourning there for miles around. A suitable spot is chosen out; and then the first necessity is to build a hide. This must not be more than four and a half feet high on the inside. A cartwheel does duty for the roof, set crosswise on the top; the entrance is a rough-and-ready kind of door, which should open towards the eastern side, since the east wind rarely brings rain. This, and indeed the whole of the hide, must be covered and thatched with turf. The turves laid just beneath the cartwheel are arranged in such a way that, if one or two are lifted off, an oblong gap is made, which serves as a peephole. The next thing is to put up two shelters for the butcher-birds[1] which are used during the trapping operation. These should be about twelve feet away from the hide, and fifteen feet apart, and consist of a sort of turf butt, five feet high and two feet across, opening towards the falconer's hide, and likewise covered with turf. Three slim rods bent into a semicircle, their ends thrust into the ground, are then set round the opening to act as perches for the butcher-birds, which are

[1] The Great Grey Shrike, *Lanius excubitor excubitor*.

A method for taking birds perched on a branch – it looks complicated, and the bird seems peculiarly unwary, but no doubt it worked once.

Nets were also strung between trees and bushes along the routes taken by migrating birds. A decoy was put out, attracting the hawk into the nets.

tied to the middle of the rounded top of their shelter by a line attached to a leather collar round their breasts. A longer rod is then bent into a bow above the other three, to prevent any passing sparrowhawk from snatching the shrikes off their perch. This done, the next thing is to drive in three twenty-foot poles, forty yards from the hide and twenty to twenty-five yards apart, to the tops of which are attached creances whose free ends lie in the hide. A live pigeon is tied by the feet to the creance on the first pole, that which stands on the right-hand side seen from the hide; and near this pole a little turf shelter is built for the pigeon. A tame hawk, whose mediocre quality renders her of no particular value for hunting, is then attached to the creance on the second pole, and on the same creance, a short distance from the hawk, is tied a large bunch of feathers. The third pole is dressed with a similar bunch of feathers and a wooden decoy hawk. And now the nets must be set up for catching the hawks. These nets, three in number, are set up a hundred yards away from the falconer's hide: one to the north-west, one to the south, the third and last to the north-east. the nets are oval in shape, and while half of the edge of the net is fixed to the rim of a wooden bow, two and a half feet in diameter, the free edge is pegged to the ground with a series of small wooden pegs. The bow is then turned back upon the half on the ground, so that the whole of the net lies beneath the bow, and the whole is then sprinkled with grass and heather. To one side of the bow is attached a wire, which runs through a little gap cut in the foot of the fal-coner's hide. In the centre of the space the net would cover, a small stake is then driven, with a hole drilled through it to take a creance, whose free end also lies in the hide. To this, a live pigeon is tied, and the pigeon shut up in a turf coop about thirty feet to the rear of the net. The coop should have a trap, made of a turf – which, when the pigeon is pulled out at the hawk's approach, falls open of its own accord. The whole apparatus for taking the hawks is now ready; and having set it up exactly as we have described, the falconer has nothing more to do than to make his way to the hide at sunrise each day, and remain there until the sun goes down. Seated in a chair in his narrow cell of turf, his eyes fixed by the hour upon

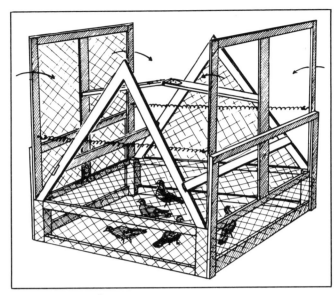

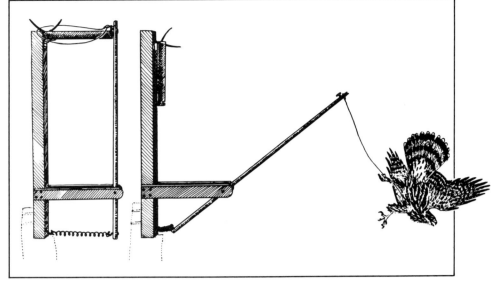

Various methods of trapping falcons. Above, left: Two American systems. In the first, pigeons are confined in a separate, lower wire-mesh cage. When a falcon tries to attack, the upper panels pivot in, releasing the pigeons, and confining the falcon in the upper 'A' shaped cage. The second is a variant of a pole trap, in which when the falcon alights on the perch, it falls, leaving the bird caught by the legs in a noose. Below: The Dutch method, see text.

Right: Modern method for trapping goshawks. A pigeon, supplied with food and water, is put in the lower compartment. When a hawk or falcon attacks, the netting upper part is sprung by the perch provided, and the pigeon escapes.

An excellent medieval illustration of training the falcon to the lure. The bird, on a creance or long line, has been called off the fist of the assistant, and is flying to the lure being swung by the falconer.

the shrikes, he may not distract himself in any way whatsoever – his only pastime being to smoke his pipe. From time to time he must shift the wooden decoy, in order to bring up the falcons and hawks from a great way off – who, believing it to be one of their kin in pursuit of prey, and spurred on by envy or the hope of finding the wherewithal to satisfy their own appetite, come flying up to investigate a spot so seemingly-attractive. As soon as a bird comes in sight, the butcher-birds will look up at the sky; the hunter then drops the decoy, a crude imitation which would never deceive a wild hawk for long, and makes haste to wake up the tame hawk on the creance in the middle, and then the pigeon tied to the creance on the right. As their enemy draws nearer, the butcher-birds show by the extent of their agitation what kind of a bird is in sight: if it is a kite, a buzzard, or an eagle, they will be only mildly worried; if a harrier, they will bate from their perch and emit their harsh alarm-cry; if, on the other hand, they see a sparrowhawk or a peregrine coming up, they will screech with fear and dive for cover into their shelter. If this signal is given, the hunter will pull out from the coop the pigeon shut up to the rear of the bow-net, for the hawk is now closing fast. The hawk at once stoops at the pigeon, catches it, and fixes her talons into it so firmly that the hunter may, by pulling on the creance, drag both at once towards the pierced stake described above, and, without further difficulty, catch them in the net. In this way all kinds of birds of prey may be taken, either in autumn or in spring, but particularly peregrines, though sometimes even gyrfalcons. The latter, however, are only rarely to be met with outside Norway, and it is usually necessary to make an expedition to their native land in order to obtain them, where they may be taken in exactly the way we have just described, by setting up bow-nets on high points in that land of hills and mountains.

There are several other ways of taking the large falcons, simpler than the preceding way, but only possible when, by a stroke of good fortune, a bird is found in suitable terrain. In such circumstances, if a hawk is sighted, an attempt must be made to close in on her unseen. Having got within reasonable distance, a pigeon is released with a three-foot line, smeared with bird-lime,[1] tied to its feet, the line being weighted on its free end with

Illustrations taken from Frederick II of Hohenstaufen's *Art of Falconry*. Left: The falconer prepares food for his bird, and feeds it on the block. Below, left: In fine weather, the falcon is allowed to weather out of doors. Above right: The falcon comes to know his master by being carried, stroked, and fed with a bechin on the fist. Centre right: The falcon being hooded. Bottom right: The trained falcon is taken out to be flown.

[1] Bird-lime is illegal in Gt. Britain.

80

a small pebble. The hawk takes the pigeon, becomes entangled in the line smeared with bird-lime, falls to the ground, and cannot get up again. The hunter may then go up and take the hawk at his leisure. The following method is normally used for recapturing lost hawks which, having tasted freedom for a time, have returned to the wild state to some extent. As soon as the hawk is sighted, a pigeon is released with a line tied to its feet perhaps sixty or eighty feet long, and so long enough to obstruct the hawk, by its weight, from carrying the pigeon when caught. By this device, the hawk is obliged to devour her prey on the ground; but no sooner has she killed and begun to break into it than the hunter appears and drives her off. A noose is then made in a line a hundred or so feet long, and the noose is put round the pigeon, the end of the line being tied to a stake driven into the ground nearby. The noose is covered with pigeon-feathers, in the case of a lost hawk, or with grass and heather in the case of a wild hawk; and the hunter then retires, hiding somewhere nearby with the free end of the line in his hand, to await the return of the hawk. The hawk, seeing no-one by, will soon return to her prey, and may then be caught by the feet in the noose, which is pulled tight by the hunter.

For trapping a goshawk, the method is somewhat different. The most common way is by means of a sort of cage in the shape of a cube wider above than below; the walls of the cage are made of coarse netting, and the top is hinged and so arranged, by means of a fairly simple mechanism, that it shuts off the opening of the cage the moment the hawk attempts to carry off the pigeon tied up within. The cage is placed on a pole driven into the ground near the edge of a wood. For taking goshawks, a square net may also be employed, suspended so as to cover a space of ten or twelve cubic feet. The goshawk seizes the pigeon tied up in the centre of the net, and becomes entangled to such an extent that all her efforts to free herself are vain. To catch brancher hawks, it is possible to call them to the net by mimicking the calls of the parent birds. Sparrowhawks, merlins, and the smaller birds of prey generally may be taken either in a finching net or in the kind known as a drawnet; but as the different methods of trapping goshawks, sparrowhawks, and the smaller species of hawk are well-known to all hunters, and as they are never used by falconers, we shall not go into them in detail here.

As soon as the bird intended for hawking has been captured, her wings must be put into a cloth sock, and she must be pinioned with the tapes attached to it. She should then be carried home. If the hawk is caught in the morning, she may be kept until evening as long as a rufter hood is put on her and her legs are fitted with jesses, the knots of which should be secured with a string. She is then brailed, her talons and beak are blunted, and she is tied up on the ground outside the hide, where she may remain until it is time to go home. The final attentions which should be given her have to do with the management and training of the hawk, and this matter we shall now discuss at length.

If the reader consults the many books which have appeared on the art of falconry, he will discover that the falconers of today have reduced the

Japanese falconer with a hooded falcon, from a print by Kyosai.

82

第四番　集頭巾
大緒
山大緒

Faucon dormant

眠鷹之図

第八番
火針
大鷹の分・
鵰の分
住み鷹
雨傘

第六番
水盤
大鷹

ねのうちみえ鷹にて
鷲捉へ
候わんす
れ
浜本如流

神の歌
うそを売己ら
餌盤宮城
あきの庵の
林を
なにん

第五番
鷹箱
餌盤
庵丁
餌板

Kyosai's prints of falconry scenes. Left: A countryman climbs a tree to take eyass (chicks) from the nest. Above left: Falcons are dried off after bathing, while one is stroked with the frisfrass. Above right: A falcon sleeps on the screen perch. Below left: Falcon is given a bath. Below right: Feeding a falcon in the travelling case.

management of hawks to the simplest essentials. They have accepted the fact that no infallible remedies exist for curing birds struck down by serious illness, and instead of going to useless lengths to try to work a cure on a sick bird, they attempt rather to prevent such sickness occurring by taking all possible care of the bird's health.

In the attainment of this end, the first requirement is a proper choice and regulation of the food given to the hawks. The normal daily ration consists of fresh beef, from which the gristle and skin as well as the fat have been removed. This is cut into pieces for short-wings, and it is fed to them on the fist; but for long-wings it should first be finely minced or hashed into a kind of paste, and one or two fresh eggs mixed into it. Eyasses are fed this meat once or twice a day, say at seven in the morning, and again at five in the afternoon, and they are allowed to eat as much as they want at each feed; but it is a good idea to let them have, as a change from the usual meat, live pigeon[1] or fresh-killed crow or jackdaw once or twice a week. It is enough if passagers, and adult hawks generally, are fed once a day; but is essential to keep to certain rules regarding the time at which they are fed and the amount of food they are given at each meal. Passage hawks just captured from the wild should be given the meat in the morning, say at ten o'clock, but they may also be allowed to pull a few bechins from a piece of meat at the end of their ordinary feeding-time, and then when they are returned to their perch after being carried on the fist between four and eleven o'clock in the evening. This system ceases as soon as we begin to teach the hawk to fly to the fist. The hawk should then be given her daily rations at one in the afternoon; but this rule need not be too strictly applied to the goshawk or the sparrowhawk. Hawks in the wild state cannot obtain fresh prey every single day, and are consequently obliged to go for a whole day without food now and again; so we should likewise vary the quantity of meat that is allowed them. It is usual to give a full gorge on Saturdays, this day being followed by the day of rest, when they may be given only half-gorge. During the flying season, the hawks are not fed until they have flown, but this rule, again, must be modified in the case of the gyrfalcon and the white and Iceland falcons. These large falcons digest their prey more slowly than other species, and thus cannot be flown two days in succession. They should be given a gorge on the day they flown, and half-gorge on the day following. As the hawks are given pigeons, during training, each time they flown or performed their exercise properly, the amount of feathers necessary to aid digestion is swallowed automatically, but when, later, they are being fed on beef again, they should be given castings at least twice a week, either of a live bird or of its unplucked skin if dead. The gyrfalcon and the white and Iceland falcons may, if they are to be flown at furred game, be given the skin of a hare or a rabbit.

There are several other points which must be borne in mind if the birds are to be kept in good condition. In fine weather, they should be weathered every day, that is, put out in the fresh air after they have cast.

[1] Using live birds for food is illegal in Gt. Britain.

To do this, eyasses may be put on block-perches; but passage hawks should be given hummocks of turf in the garden or some other suitable weathering-ground. The hummocks should be about a foot high, and the hooded birds should be tied by the leash to pegs or stakes driven very securely into the middle of them.

Hawks should also be given a bath from time to time. For this, they should be given a good crop and then be taken, brailed, to the bank of a river or a clear pond, where they are put down on the ground, with the creance attached to their leash, and unhooded. The falconer should then retire a short distance away. After they have bathed, the hawks should be given time to preen and get dry, but as soon as they show signs of growing restive, the falconer should make in to them cautiously, take them on the fist, hood them, and carry them home. In the case of eyasses, the bath may be given in a wide earthenware or wooden tub. During training, the hawks should be given a bath once a week, but once they are made they should only be given a bath once every three weeks.

The management of hawks during the moult requires a good deal of care, and it is customary, at the approach of the moulting season, to keep only the rare species and the particularly promising birds. As soon as they begin to drop their feathers, they should be put, three or four together, in a spacious mews provided with block-perches. Their jesses, bells, and hoods are removed; they are given plentiful daily rations and frequent baths – in a word, they are given such careful and watchful treatment as will encourage the development of the new feathers and maintain the much-valued creatures in good health. If the birds rouse and tremble, it is a sign that they are sickening for something, and this is most likely to happen during the critical period of the moult. It is then imperative to redouble the care taken of them, and to give them live pigeon in place of their normal ration of meat; this is the only piece of pharmacological wisdom the falconers of today place any reliance upon, and this is the medicine that has taken the place of the vast array of doses and pills used by their colleagues in days gone by.

Falconers have devised simple but ingenious methods of putting right any accidental damage that may occur to a bird's plumage. If a feather is broken or damaged, the damaged portion is cut off and replaced with a corresponding feather from the same species of hawk, cut so as to fit the damaged feather perfectly when the two are joined. The imping-needle is given a preliminary dip in brine or vinegar, and is then fixed first into the new feather, then in the bird's own, the bird meanwhile being held on the fist of an assistant. We do not think it would serve any useful purpose here to discuss the injuries which may be sustained by hawks. If these are light, they will heal of themselves; if the injury is to a vital part, or if the bird breaks her wing, her thigh, or her leg, she is unlikely to be fit to fly again even if she should recover.

It often happens that hawks are troubled by lice. To get rid of these, an infusion of tobacco juice and brandy is used. The beak, the nape, the wing-joints, the rump and the feet are moistened with the liquid, and the

A splendid peregrine falcon, belled, jessed and hooded, perched on its master's glove.

vermin are teased out by the smoke, to die the instant they touch the parts moistened by the liquid. Care must be taken not to damage the bird's feathers; and it is wise to press into service a couple of assistants for the first part of the operation, which is known as 'washing the bird' – one to cast and hold the bird on a cushion on a table; the other, standing at the left-hand side, to hold her feet. Two persons will be enough to carry out the second part of the operation, known as 'smoking the bird' – one to stand before, one to stand behind the bird, which may be tied to the perch. For this operation, a clay pipe is used, of which half the stem should be cut off. The pipe is filled with a light tobacco, and the bowl wrapped in a piece of cotton waste. The pipe is then lit. The bowl is held to the mouth, and the smoke blown out through the stem, which is inserted among the feathers.

We have already said that it is usual to cope the talons and beak of newly-caught hawks; this operation is usually done again, three times a year, or whenever these parts have grown so sharp that they might inflict too deep a wound on the falconer's hand, or the herons used for training and which are later to be set free, or of course upon another hawk, if the birds are disposed to crab instead of pursuing the quarry.

The mews or hawk-house should be spacious enough for the number of hawks it is proposed to keep there. The windows of the mews should have shutters, which may be closed as soon as it grows dark and opened in the morning as soon as the birds have cast. This room should be provided with screen-perches placed three or four feet away from the walls and about five feet from the floor, which underneath the perches should be covered with a thick layer of sand. The perches are usually about two and a half inches in diameter, wadded with straw and covered with coarse linen of flannel; a cloth, about two feet wide, hangs down from the perch in order to prevent the hawks, when bating, from getting their jesses twisted round the perch. If more than one hawk is put on a perch, it is wise to keep them a good two feet apart. Perches for eyasses, for sick birds, and for all birds undergoing the moult, are known as block-perches; these blocks are approximately one foot high, and wider at the base than at the top, where they should be about nine inches across; and they have a ring set in the middle to take the end of the leash when the hawk is tied up. When these blocks are used for eyasses, they are covered with turf. Each hawk has her own name written on a label attached to her perch. The mews also serves as a harness-room for all the falconer's furniture and equipment. Short-wings are not kept indoors, but on perches somewhere outside where they are sheltered from the rain, and it is important to keep them in places where there is a certain amount of to-ing and fro-ing, so as to accustom them to the presence of men and dogs.

The art of training hawks has throughout history been regarded as a noble and absorbing occupation, displaying to the very highest degree that dominion which may be acquired by mankind over the brute creation. If the training of a gun-dog is regarded as a triumph of the human over the animal, the art of training birds for hunting should surely excite even greater admiration; in the first case, the animal is a domestic one, tractable

Above: Peregrine attached to a log in the field.

Right: Merlin on the block.

90

in his nature, gregarious by instinct; whereas in the second case, we have to do with a creature newly caught from the wild, who ranks, among intelligent creatures, far lower than the dog, and whose nature is wild, fierce, and solitary. If we reflect, however, on the motives which lead both these creatures to obey the will of their master, we shall see that they are quite different in nature, even though the effects achieved in each case may be very similar. To prove the truth of this remark, we need only to compare the gun-dog and the hawk, and look a little more closely at the disposition and mental abilities of each.

The dog, both in the primitive state and when, having been domesticated, he is returned to the wild, lives in a pack. He has the gregarious instinct, and a kind of predisposition to become attached to man; he is very easily able to take to a vegetarian diet; and he has always been man's chosen companion among animals. Man, on his part, has over the years cultivated those qualities in the dog that he has found most useful, and has in so doing contributed to the changes in the dog's nature. Observing that, of all the senses, that of scent, or smell, supplies the strongest support for that natural instinct that leads the dog to seek out and pursue game, man has gradually bred the different breeds of gun-dog, among which the pointer or setter takes first place, for that is the breed in which training can be brought to the greatest degree of perfection.

If we now turn to the natural propensities of hawks, we shall find the exact opposite of all that we have just noted about the nature of the dog. Birds in general, and the hawk family in particular, occupy a much lower place than dogs and the other mammalia in the scheme of creation, and though they surpass the dog in their wonderfully keen sight, they can by no means be compared to him in their scent, which is as far as the hawk is concerned of less importance altogether. Hawks have no predisposition to become attached to man, and never feel the need for such attachment. Each individual bird has the ability to fend for itself, and these birds do, generally, lead solitary lives, uniting in pairs only when the instinct of procreation, not that of sociability, drives them on. Endowed with great strength, and living exclusively on live prey, these creatures are deadly, voracious, and wild. As they never breed in captivity, the race as a whole remains free – the isolated individuals which falconers succeed in manning never hesitating to return to the wild if they have to, or if ever they find an opportunity of killing for themselves, for they serve man neither out of affection nor of their own free will. Once set free, they will find food, no matter where they are. The man-wrought changes on the earth's surface do not hinder their primitive way of life, for they are not, like a dog, so to speak attached to the ground, but live in an element which sets no limit to their liberty, their wings giving them the freedom to flit in an instant from one place to another in search of the conditions necessary to their existence.

It follows from all this that, as the hawk does not possess those domestic, docile traits which man has bred into the dog to make him a useful helpmeet, she is simply not amenable to the kind of training given to a

Goshawk on a bow perch.

gun-dog. There is no way of making her obey her master and carry out his wishes, except by making use of that instinct which is strongest in the hawk family: that is, their appetite. Birds of prey have a habit of devouring a large quantity of food at a time, which makes them, for some time afterwards, too sluggish and heavy to be flown at fresh quarry. This characteristic has pointed man the way to gain control over the bird; he has learned to use this dominant passion for his own ends, to the point at which, if they are set free, the birds do not at once realize it, and will, in order to satisfy their appetite, stoop at quarry indicated to them, even though it may be a creature they would not naturally pursue at all; and will even let themselves be taken up again if they are offered some of their favourite food.

To sum up what we have been saying with regard to the dog and the hawk: the dog, as we have seen, serves his master from affection, obeys

Right: Peregrine falcon with tirings (left), with a sore goshawk mantling over her prey.

him of his own free will, or through fear of punishment, follows him everywhere, prefers him to any other, and never leaves him of his own accord; in pursuing game he is acting by instinct, and once the quarry has been killed, he goes to retrieve it and carries it to his master without expecting or receiving a reward of any kind; finally, once he has been trained to the sport, he will never forget the lessons he has learned, or if – led astray by his instincts – he were to forget them for a second, a reminder will suffice to call him back to his duty.

The hawk, on the other hand, feels no affection either for man in general or for her own master; she does not obey him of her own free will, and in serving his pleasure believes she is merely satisfying her own needs; punishment has not the slightest effect on her; she flies away if ever she tastes freedom for an hour or so; in flying at quarry she is not so much impelled by instinct as aware that catching the quarry will result in having meat to eat; she never returns to her master of her own free will, and in order to take her up again he has to lure her by the offer of her favourite food; finally, she only remembers the lessons she has been taught as long as they are constantly repeated. If ever she spends a few days at liberty,

those lessons have to be practised afresh before she can be used for hunting, and a longer period of time, as during the moult, for instance, is enough to make her forget all she has learned, so that her training must be renewed from the beginning if she is to be used for hunting afterwards.

Once this difference between the nature of the dog and that of the hawk has been thoroughly grasped, we shall see at once that for training birds of prey quite different methods must be employed from those used for training gun-dogs. In training gun-dogs, everything depends on the selection of the individual dog: he is of no use of he has not a keen nose. The first lesson in his education is to teach him to retrieve the game and obey his master's instructions as they are called to him. As he seeks out game by instinct, all that is needed is to repress his natural desire to devour the game, or to pursue it before he has been told to. There are no visible signs by which a hawk's qualities may be discerned. In training her for the chase, it is first necessary to tame her wild, shy nature by carrying her incessantly on the fist and manning her to the presence of men and dogs; as soon as she is manned, the preliminary lessons teach the bird, through hunger, to come to the fist when meat is offered her. When training her to fly at game, she must always be made to practise the exercise when sharp-set, and rewarded after each flight with a portion of meat. Finally, it is imperative to enter each individual bird only to the species of game she is to be flown at. These general indications will reveal the fact that the training of hawks is based on quite simple principles, and that the theory of the art may be learnt quite quickly. However, when it comes to putting that theory into practice, it soon becomes clear that long experience is required before the desired result can be guaranteed, and that it is no less difficult to train a hawk to fly at game than to control her on the wing, once she has been slipped at a quarry. Hence the art is not one that can be practised by any but professional falconers, unless we are willing to run the risk of spoiling or losing a hawk.

But it is not merely his skill in the training and flying of hawks which makes a good falconer. To merit such a title he must possess a wealth of other qualities besides. First and foremost, a falconer must be dedicated to his trade body and soul; he must have no vices; he must care for his birds with the greatest devotion, even, when necessary, sacrificing his own comfort and well-being to theirs; he should ponder upon his work, so as to discover those thousand and one little tricks and contrivances that, in order to achieve success in any endeavour, he must known how and when to apply. Independently of these qualities, the falconer will need a robust constitution, capable of enduring fatigue; patience under many trials, and that adaptability of character which is required when dealing with men of all ranks of society. Lastly, he should not be overfond of one particular branch of his art in preference to others – that is, capturing the wild birds, caring for them, training them, and flying them – unless the falconers of one company or club agree among themselves to share out these different occupations.

When selecting hawks, falconers notice, first and foremost, their age, giving the preference to young birds because they are more easily trained than the older ones; these latter being killed off as soon as the requisite number of young birds has been obtained. These, too, are usually destroyed at the end of the flying season, when they are about to enter their second year, as it is customary to keep only the rare species of hawk, and the individuals who have shown good flying qualities, to moult in captivity. The selection of the bird depends both upon the kind of hawking she is to be used for, and the opportunities of procuring the species concerned. However, passagers are wherever possible to be preferred to eyasses, for all birds lose condition in captivity, more especially those which have been reared in captivity.

The training of birds of prey, as we have seen, is based upon certain immutable principles; and it follows that, though the general method of training applies to all birds, many modifications must be introduced according to the species we are trying to train, according to whether the bird was taken from the nest or from the wild, and according to the kind of hawking she is to be used for. Before we go into the details of the training of hawks proper, however, we should first discuss the management of

Peregrine falcon on the fist.

the young birds from the time they are removed from the nest until they are full-grown and consequently ready to be trained for flying at quarry.

For eyass hawks, there is only one system of upbringing. The main points to bear in mind are: to give them abundance of food of the first quality; to ensure that the most perfect cleanliness reigns in the hackhouse; to allow them their liberty for as long as possible – in a word, to do everything possible to favour the full development of their plumage and their powers of flight. Their makeshift eyrie may be made of a large basket, four or five feet deep, set on its side in a quiet corner of the grounds, within reach of the hand, in the branches of a tree, with the basket's opening facing south. The basket may be covered with turves to keep out the rain, with a thick thatch of straw inside to serve the same purpose. The lid of the basket should be opened out flat, to form a table or hack-board. If we follow, with regard to their rations, the rules we laid down when discussing the management of hawks generally, the eyasses will soon have grown to the point of quitting their eyrie and perching in the branches of trees, or on housetops, gradually undertaking longer flights, but always returning of their own accord as long as their food is put out regularly and in plentiful supply. They are left at liberty in this way until the day when they first obtain their own food by killing birds or other animals; and that is the moment at which to take them up, which is usually done by means of the kind of bow-net used for taking passage hawks. If we wish to hack eyasses which have already been flown, before recommencing their training, it is essential to attach a heavy leaden bell to each of their feet, so as to prevent their killing for themselves; and it is also necessary to nail down their meat on to the hack-board, for unless this is done they will carry the meat and devour it elsewhere – a habit common to nearly all falcons, and which must be stamped out at the start if we are to prevent the bird from turning into a confirmed carrier when out flying. Eyass hawks are not used for heron and kite hawking, and their training is shorter amd simpler than that of passage hawks, upon which subject we shall now say a few words, before entering into the further details of the training of eyasses.

As soon as a newly-caught passage hawk has been brought in, she should be put in a dark room and left tied to a block covered with turf until the following day. We must not forget, this first night, to unhood her, so that she can cast. The first task is to accustom her to being fed from the fist. To do this, we take her on the gloved fist, and offer her a piece of meat, which she is allowed to pull at and eat, bit by bit. A few will be enough to have her manned to the point of taking her food with avidity, and from this moment the meat that makes up her daily ration should be cut into strips, not too large for her to swallow comfortably. If she bates violently when we take her on the fist, the brail may be used, and she may also be quietened by splashing her feathers with water, or even dipping her into a bucket of cold water.[1] She is not unhooded for a moment during this

[1] I cannot find out if this disgusting and barbarous practice is illegal or not. As far as I can make out, it is not.

early part of her training, and she is not given castings of feathers or fur, for this period, as she cannot cast with her hood on. This period may, according to whether the hawk is of reserved or docile temperament, last four or five days. As soon as she takes the meat she is given quite readily, and will stay quietly on the fist, she is replaced on her perch and her rufter hood changed for the ordinary hood, which must be removed nightly in order to allow her to cast; for after this first period of manning she should be given the occasional pigeon or other animal with its feathers or fur. The next task is to overcome her shyness by carrying her on the fist twice a day, in the morning and afternoon, for several hours at a stretch, inside the house. Then she should be taken outside, and then when there are people passing to and fro; she may also be unhooded now and again, given a few bechins of meat, and then rehooded, until she becomes accustomed, gradually, to take meat unhooded, and to pull at the pieces of meat presented to her. During this period, she may be stroked from time to time with a pigeon's wing, for birds do not like to be touched with the hand. Having handled her in this way for a week or thereabouts, the preliminary training sessions may be begun, though she must still be carried on the fist regularly every day. In fact, hawks should be carried on the fist twice a day the whole year round, to keep them from becoming wild and discourage them from putting on weight. During the flying season, when the hawks are carried out to the field every day on the cadge, this exercise need only be done if we are prevented from going out for more than a couple of days by bad weather or other circumstances.

The first training proper should be given in the middle of the day, and it consists of teaching the hawk to jump to the fist of her own volition. For this, she should be placed on the back of a chair; the end of the leash is then twined round the little finger of the falconer's gloved left hand, and a piece of meat is held in the right hand; having unhooded the bird (the hood being retained in the little finger of the right hand), the hands are brought together, and, standing close to her, the falconer should offer her the piece of meat and coax her to come to the fist for it, whistling to her the while. If she comes to the fist, she is permitted a few bechins; then replaced on the chair, and again made to come to the fist. This exercise is repeated four or five times on that day, and after the lesson is over, the bird is given a good crop. Increasing the distance she must come each day, the leash is finally taken off, and the hawk encouraged to fly free the whole length of the room to the falconer's fist. This exercise should be repeated over a period of two or three weeks, after which a new series of lessons is begun, introducing the hawk to a pigeon on a creance. For these lessons the hawk is kept on the leash; then a creance is attached to the leash, and she is allowed to pursue the pigeon all round the room, being encouraged to stoop at it by a cry, or shout, repeated over and over again. It is, of course, essential to let the hawk eat the pigeon when she catches it, so that this lesson can only be practised once a day. When the hawk is confident at this exercise, which may take as little as three days or as long as two weeks, her lessons may take place in the open. On the first day she should

be taken out to the country in the morning to have her bath, and after returning to the mews, we should wait until noon before unhooding her, making her jump to the fist, and giving her a good crop, after which she may be left alone until the following day. We then take her out again, and repeat the lesson with the pigeon, which is released on a creance, first a short, then a longer, distance away, the distance being increased gradually to about twenty paces. Finally, the pigeon is released on the creance and the assistant holding it is told to run at full speed. Two or three weeks will suffice for this exercise, but during the second week, the hawk should be given her lesson only every other day, her diet being altered to give her a large gorge on the day she is flown, and half-gorge the day after, which should be spent in repeating the exercise of flying to the fist. Passage peregrines are usually trained to fly large game, so it is important to enter her next to a fowl on a creance, instead of the pigeon, the creance not being more than about fifteen feet long. After one or two weeks at this exercise, the fowl should be replaced by a cock, and the hawk should be entered to this, and practised until she is perfectly confident and will attack the cock regardless of its flapping and squawking. This will usually take from two to four, sometimes as long as six, weeks, and it goes without saying that the

A peregrine falcon leaving the glove.

A merlin coming to the fist.

hawk is rewarded each time she attacks the cock by being given a live pigeon. Two weeks may then be spent in going over all the lessons in turn, in the open if the weather is fine, or in the yard or inside the mews if it is too wet or windy outside. This done, a further two weeks should be spent at the exercise of flying a pigeon, the difference being that this time the hawk flies free, that is, not on the creance; whereas the pigeon is still held on a line. These final lessons must be absorbed, and then we must turn to teaching the hawk to fly in a cast, that is, in company with another hawk. The two birds should first be made to fly at the pigeon on the creance; then a line about twenty or so feet long is tied to the pigeon's feet, in order to slow it down and prevent it from flying away altogether, and at each succeeding lesson, part of the line is removed, so that it ends up about five feet long. Once the hawks are accustomed to flying in a cast and returning to the lure when offered it with live bait, then the training may be said to be completed, the entire programme of lessons having taken up perhaps four or five months. We may now continue the training by entering the hawk to the kind of quarry for which she is intended.

We propose to deal first of all with the method of training hawks for heron-hawking. For this, only the white falcon, the Iceland falcon, the

gyrfalcon and the passage peregrine can be used. But the first necessity is to procure the heron. They are usually taken by putting a running knot or noose round their nest sometime towards dusk, the hunter then hiding downwind about twenty paces from the tree containing the nest, the free end of the line carrying the noose being kept in his hand. This is pulled tight as the heron lands on the nest. Once caught, the bird's eyes should be seeled, and it is then shut up in a dark shed. The operation of seeling is done as follows: a fine thread is threaded through the lower lid of each eye by means of a sewing-needle, the threads being then twisted together on top of the heron's head so that the eyelids are drawn up to cover the entire eyeball. Herons in captivity almost always refuse food, and in this case they must be force-fed each day by having a few morsels of meat pushed down their throat and a glass of water poured down after them. It may even prove necessary to stop the heron regurgitating the meat it has been given by tying a cord round the upper part of its neck. For the initial lessons in flying heron, a field or a piece of open ground not too far away should be selected, and the hawks, together with the heron, taken out there. One falconer then sets the heron down; kneeling on his left knee, he unseels it, puts on the beak shield, throws a scarf over its head, and holds it so that it is unable to move. A little to the rear of the first falconer, and on his left, stands a second falconer with a hawk on his fist, while behind him again stands a third falconer, also carrying a hawk, so that the training may be carried on without a break. All being arranged just as we have described, the lesson is begun by the first falconer releasing the heron, which finds itself held by a long creance; the second falconer at once unhoods the hawk he is holding (also on a creance) and casts her at the heron. She flies straight at the heron, and as soon as she binds to it, the falconers make in as quickly as they can and offer her a live pigeon, which she is encouraged to eat while still holding the heron in her feet. For these lessons the same rules should be observed regarding the distance the heron is allowed to fly, as were laid down for the lessons with the pigeon. After a couple of weeks, these exercises may with advantage be repeated a few times more on more extensive ground such as, for instance, a heath or moor; the hawk is then flying free, and the heron is not on a creance but is simply tied by the foot to a twenty-foot line, so as to hinder him from mounting too high. The two or three succeeding lessons are given over to flying the hawks at the heron in a cast – the heron now being loose. After this, the hawks should be taken out in the afternoon to a moor in the vicinity of a heronry, to await the herons who are flying home after fishing for food. Being gorged with fish, the herons will fly low and slowly towards their home wood, and during these early days it is desirable to enter the hawks to low-flying herons so as to build up their confidence before they are entered to those flying high. This series of lessons in flying at herons will take about two months, and the preliminary training, as we have seen, takes four to five months, so we should calculate on a period of six or seven months being necessary to enter hawks successfully at bagged heron.

For entering the hawk to kites, the procedure is exactly the same, the

A falcon stooping to the lure, which is being swung beneath it. The jesses trail behind the feet.

sole difference being that a kite instead of a heron is used during the final series of lessons. The best hawks for flying kite are the white and Iceland falcons, the gyrfalcon, and the saker; the sakret and the passage peregrine may also be used, though with less hope of success.

If it is intended to enter the hawk to hare and rabbit, she must first be taught to fly a pigeon, a fowl, and a cock, exactly as was done in the case of the hawks intended for heron and kite-hawking. Once the preparatory training is finished, a hare's pelt stuffed with hay should be dragged across the floor of the mews on a string, the hawk being cast at it on a creance. As soon as the bird has gained experience at this part of the training, it should be repeated in the field, the hare's pelt being dragged, slowly at first, then faster, by a boy running full tilt, and then by a groom on horseback dragging it at the gallop; during this stage, of course, the hawk is flying free. This entire series of lessons is then begun all over again, the hare's pelt being replaced by a live, tame hare bred on the estate, which is finally allowed to run free. The peregrine, the saker, and the jerkin have not the strength to fly hares, and only the white and Iceland falcons, and the gyrfalcon, should be used. Owing to their greater strength, however, these large species are more likely than any to turn carrier. To nip this habit in the bud they should be taught to fly down, by using the lure, to a piece of meat nailed to a plank placed on the ground, and this exercise should be repeated in the field every time the birds fall back into the same fault. For the same reason, the live pigeon used for training should always be held on a line.

The training of eyass hawks is not by any means as long or as problematical as that of passage hawks. Not only are they manned more easily (being raised in captivity they are less shy than the wild-caught hawk), but during their first year at least they cannot be used for heron and kite-hawking. The main difference between the training of passage hawks and eyasses is that the latter are never lured with live bait, only with the lure; that only pigeons, never fowls or cocks, are used for training and that they are taught to wait on – that is, to climb up before the game is flushed and wait overhead, while the falconers and dogs work below. Eyasses are trained in this way: the moment they are fully developed, they are netted, or taken up; and then hooded, jessed, and belled, taken to their quarters and tied to their blocks; after which the falconer withdraws for a few hours. He then returns to the mews, takes the hawk on his fist to accustom her to staying there without bating, and carries her on the fist twice a day, in the customary fashion, for several hours at a stretch, treating her just like a passage hawk. As soon as she is manned thus far, she should be taught to jump from her block to the fist. Next, a piece of meat is thrown down on the ground, and she is allowed to pull at it, being then recalled to the fist and given her daily ration of meat. When she has grasped these lessons, she should be entered to the lure, which should be presented to her, attractively baited, first a short way away and then gradually further off, so that she must jump or stoop at the lure to get at the bait. In the succeeding lessons, the lure is thrown down on the ground, first quite near to her, then each day, a little further off, and finally as far away from her as possible. The falconer must take care to make in to her gently when she is eating the meat on the lure and walk slowly round her in a circle, whistling. Once she has absorbed these lessons, the last of which may be given in the open, she may be taken on the fist out to some open ground. An assistant should be in position to begin to swing the lure for her, a short distance away. The creance is removed, and the hawk is slipped at it, but as she approaches the lure, it is jerked up into the air, in such a way that the bird does not collide with it, nor seize it before it falls to the ground. This exercise must be repeated several times, following which the lure is held in the hand instead of being thrown up, and the instant the hawk stoops at it, the lure is twitched away so that she passes it by. She should be called to at the same time. As soon as it is clear that the hawk is growing discouraged, the lure is thrown up and the hawk allowed to catch and eat the meat upon it. It is also wise to change position when swinging the lure to accustom her to following the falconer's movements as she flies; but we must stop practising this lesson the moment she has grasped it, for otherwise there is a danger of her picking up the habit of flying low, which would be most undesirable in a bird intended for partridge-hawking. When the hawk has been sufficiently rehearsed at this exercise, she must be taught to recognize the kind of quarry she is to be flown at. With this aim in mind, we should move out to the field with her and cast her off, while an assistant, stationed some distance away, slips a bird of the species we wish to enter her to. If, during the preparatory lessons, the quarry has always been held on a line, and the hawk rewarded regularly for catching it, she will soon be sufficiently trained to that quarry. For partridge, crow, magpie, duck, and other birds, eyass hawks are the best birds to use; but if, for want of a passage bird, an eyass is to be flown at heron and kite, it is best to select an intermewed eyass and train her in exactly the same way as a passage hawk.

The merlin has a friendly nature and may ordinarily be fully made in three to four weeks; she need only be hooded when first caught, while being carried home. She is manned by carrying her on the fist in the usual daily routine, and once she will fly to the fist, she should be made to do this again in the open, first being put down on a tree-branch, tied to the creance, and then flying free. After a couple of weeks, she may be entered to quarry, the falconer proceeding in precisely the same was as was described for eyasses. The merlin may be used for flights at all sorts of small birds, especially for larks, but also for snipe, plover, and similar game. She is often flown in a cast, that is, two birds are flown at the quarry at once, and in olden times it appears that a merlin was often used to encourage the hawks being flown at a heron to mount well.

The making of the goshawk demands much less skill than is required for falcons. Branchers are generally to be preferred to eyasses or passagers. With regard to the training of eyass goshawks, the same rules should be followed as for eyass falcons; and brancher and passage goshawks need not be hooded, except for the first few days after capture; for the goshawk, like all the hawks of the fist, is slower on the wing than the falcon, so she needs to see the quarry, and stoop at it the instant it gets up. The goshawk should be manned to noise as early as possible, and as it is usual to keep only one or two of these hawks at a time, they may well be kept in close proximity to men and dogs, in a fairly busy spot. For weathering purposes, it is wise to put up a perch between two trees in a garden or somewhere not unfrequented. The goshawk's jesses have, as we have seen, an additional attachment known as the shortleash, which is a sort of prolongation of the jess. Its use is to enable the goshawk, who is inclined to bate frequently off the perch, to climb back on to it. It is easier to detach than the swivel, and so the bird may be more quickly leashed than if wearing ordinary jesses. Conversely, the shortleash is never used for falcons, for these birds must not be given too much room on the perch or cadge, in case they try to injure one another or damage their feathers. When beginning the goshawk's training, it is most important to man her thoroughly by much carrying on the fist. During these carrying sessions, she may be allowed to take a few bechins now and again from the lure or from a piece of meat presented to her on the fist. She should then be taught to jump to the fist, from the ground as well as from the perch, or a tree-branch, daily jumping a longer distance. To call her, the falconer should show her the lure or a piece of meat, and whistle to her. Once she has advanced to this stage, she may be entered to quarry. The goshawk is used only for partridge-hawking, so it will suffice if she is made to fly a few times at a tame partridge, first held on a string, then released in the open. If the goshawk should be required for rabbit-hawking, she may be trained by entering her first to a tame rabbit, and after a few practice flights at this, by setting her at a wild rabbit served to her.

The sparrowhawk is made in exactly the same way as the goshawk, but she should be given ordinary jesses. The musket is rarely used for hawking. It is sometimes possible to train the sparrowhawk in under a fortnight. She is usually flown at young partridge, quail, corncrake, and other sorts of small birds.

Only very seldom have eagles been used for hawking in this country. This is partly because of the difficulty of procuring them, partly also because Europe lacks the kinds of large game that would be suited to them, at least in the open country where hawking is practised. There is the further disadvantage that eagles are to heavy to be carried on the fist. Only land eagles can be used for hawking, that is, the species whose feet are feathered to the toes. Eyass eagles are to be preferred, and these are trained to wait on over dogs, in the same way as when eyass peregrines are flown at partridge.

When out in the field, all hawks are held on their jesses, which, like their bells, are never removed from their feet even when flying; so when using ordinary field jesses, before the birds are cast off, their swivel and leash must be removed. With the goshawk, however, only the shortleash need be taken off, this being left on the leash, which is then clipped on to the hawking bag while the bird is being flown.

A falcon that has bound to the lure. The falconer next makes in to his bird, offering a bechin as a reward, and distracting his falcon's attention from the lure.

106

A seventeenth-century engraving by Johan Stradan, showing an idealized hawking party having an extraordinarily successful day at heron. Falcons flown at heron was thought to be the most spectacular form of the sport.

the different forms of hawking

Of all forms of hawking, none presents a more magnificent spectacle than the sport of heron or kite-hawking with noble falcons. This has been held in higher esteem than any other form of hawking, from the earliest times down to our own day; and it is the only form of hawking to be worthy of the name *vol royal* – the royal flight. However, as the kite is a far rarer bird than the heron, being found, even in its best-known haunts, in relatively small numbers, it is hardly possible to indulge in the sport of kite-hawking alone. This is also true of heron-hawking in localities where these birds are found only in small numbers, rather than congregating in large heronries, for then isolated individuals must be sought out. But in districts where large heronries are found in the midst of open downland or heath (not ploughland, for we must be able to ride freely across country), then heron-hawking may take place on the proper scale and in the time-honoured manner, for several months in succession. Heron-hawking is undeniably a noble and splendid sport; no other kind of hawking can be compared with it. But now that there are not many large heronries left, and even those often surrounded either by marsh or by ploughland, there remain only a few places in Europe which combine all the conditions necessary for heron-hawking, and none which can offer them combined to such advantage as in Holland.

Mounted falconer about to fly his falcon, an engraving by J. E. Riedinger.

The hawking season begins in June, when the young heron are full-grown, and lasts until about the end of July, when the hawks begin their moult. In selecting the venue to await the herons, the direction of the wind is the first thing to look to, it being imperative, for reasons which we shall go into later, to take up position downwind, or at a point which is exposed to the wind blowing across the heronry. The distance away from the latter may vary, according to the nature of the ground, from half a mile to five miles, or sometimes even further. As the nature of the ground dictates, certain particular spots will be chosen to fly the hawks from, and so it will be possible to put up a rough bothy, or even a couple of bothies, to shelter the field in case of rain: that is, the hunters, the hawks, and perhaps the

A lithograph of a Eastern gazelle hunt, using goshawks to slow down the animal until the dogs come up. The Bedouins of the desert have been famous for centuries for their skill in training falcons. From Burton's *Falconry in the Valley of the Indus.*

On the continent, falconry was a privilege reserved for nobles, and many a squire, too poor perhaps to afford to keep his pack, went hunting with hawk, dog, and a single retainer.

A mounted falconer following a heron. The best sport was shown by a heron on passage, that is, flying between its feeding ground and the heronry. The falconer tried to place himself between the heron and the heronry before flying his falcon.

Pheasants make good quarry for both peregrines and goshawks. A tough old cock pheasant can give a good account of himself when attacked by a gos or a peregrine, making for a sporting contest.

horses as well. The best time to go out to the field is in the afternoon, between four o'clock and dusk. The falconers and their assistants, on horseback and accompanied by the cadge-boys, repair to the flying area in advance, and tie the falcons being used to stakes driven into the ground. All necessary preparations are made, and when the rest of the field rides up, an assistant falconer or groom goes out to get into position as look-out, a good half-mile downwind, on a slight rise where he can be seen and from which he has a good view of all the herons coming from that direction. Two falconers, mounted with falcons on fist, also take up position a few hundred yards from the hawking party, in the direction of the heronry. The moment the downwind look-out sees a heron he thinks may be flown, he alerts the field by getting off his horse and turning its head in the

111

direction the heron is coming from. At this signal, the general cry of 'A flight!' is heard, and all eyes turn to gaze at the part of the sky the heron is coming from. Everyone in the party throws himself on to his horse to get to a good vantage-point for watching the spectacle, though taking care not to affright the heron by making too much noise. The falconers move as near to the heron as they can get without turning it from the direction it is flying in. They await the right moment, moving in as close as seems feasible. They let the heron pass overhead, and as soon as it has gone a few hundred yards they unhood and cast the falcons. Despite the fact that the falcons at first fly low, and in opposite directions, diverging without appearing to make for the heron, the latter is at once aware that he is their chosen quarry. Instantly, he stretches out his neck, disgorges his cropful of fish so as to reduce his weight, and flies for his life towards the heronry or some nearby cover. The falcons ring up so as to be able to close on the heron. The heron, unable to gain on them and knowing well that they can only stoop at him from above, has only one hope: to soar up. But he cannot do this against the wind, and is thus forced to change direction and start to fly towards the falcons, the head-start he was given by the falcons not being cast at once, now being reversed to the falcons' advantage. And now the three birds, who began by flying in different directions, converge at incredible speed. Now the attention of the hawking party is riveted to the events overhead, all eyes are on the birds, and each member of the party tries to keep as close to the flight as possible. The heron, uttering frequent plaintive cries, is still making every effort to soar up as high as he can so as to escape downwind. But the falcons pursue him keenly, and as soon as one of them gets within reach of him, she at once stoops, the heron trying to evade her stoop by jinking. If he escapes her feet, he may still be thrust forty feet or more earthwards by the violence of the blow – but now, the other falcon in the cast, whose flight has not been checked by an attack, has reached the same height as the heron, and stoops at him in her turn. If she misses, it is again the turn of the first, and they will keep up these alternating stoops, turn by turn, until one or other of the falcons succeeds in binding to the prey, usually gripping him by the neck or one wing. At this point, the other falcon joins her comrade, and the three birds together are then seen to descend through the air quite slowly, as if the three were one. Before they pitch on the ground, one of the cast generally leaves go, and the other will do the same if there is a risk of her hitting the ground; though she will seize her prey again the instant it touches the ground or shows signs of escaping. The falconers, who have given their horses their heads in the effort to keep up with the flight, gallop up the instant the birds bring the heron down, rather tumbling than dismounting from their horses, and while one of them offers the falcon who let go the prey a pigeon on the lure, the other makes in circumspectly, takes hold of the heron by his neck, and gives the second falcon a pigeon too, which she will break into with her feet still gripping the heron. The falcons are allowed a good crop, and are then hooded and carried back to the hawking party. As for the heron, if he has not been either killed outright or mortally wounded,

This painting by Claude Dervet, symbolising 'Air',
comes from the Château de Richelieu. Quite apart
from its allegory, the picture shows how brilliant a
spectacle a noble hawking party could be.

he is usually set free; but if, for instance, he should be required for training purposes, then he is tied up, and either seeled or hooded. His beak is
muzzled by the beak shield, for it is at this point that herons seek to defend
themselves by striking about with their beaks, not, as is generally supposed, during the flight. During this interval, two other falconers have
taken up their positions, with fresh falcons, so that flights may be had at
all the herons which happen to pass over the hunting ground that day.
Although the procedure for each flight is roughly the same, the changing
circumstances give rise to much variety of sport. If the heron is empty –
that is to say, if it has not eaten, it will very often ring into the clouds, and
with it the falcons, and in such a case will in all probability get away. If
on the other hand it is full-gorged with fish, and is flying low, it may happen
that one of the falcons will take it in her first stoop. If there is a good deal
of wind, it is often only possible for the hawking party to follow the flight
at all by strenuous riding, and the spectacle may only be seen from a dis-

Eugène Fromentin painted falconry scenes in the Algerian desert in the middle of the nineteenth century, witnessing the perennial love for this sport among the Arabs. Above, a cast of falcons attack a crane. Below: The falconers make in to the falcon and its quarry.

tance. Besides, there is some risk of losing the falcons if the flight takes place towards dusk, in failing light, and any such loss is the more felt, in that it is usually the best falcons who disappear – a good falcon being tireless in pursuit, as long as the quarry does not put into cover. Herons, particularly, always try to gain either the nearest wood or the nearest patch of water, into which they will plummet to safety. To enjoy the finest flights, and to be able to watch them in comfort, the weather should be still, with no wind to speak of, and the herons old and strong. They should not fly low in order to disgorge their food and make themselves lighter in weight, but should, ideally, mount straight up.

There are many other delights which add to the pleasures of heron-hawking. The surrounding vista of the wide stretches of heath-clothed moorland, lit by the straying gleams of the sun; now hiding his face behind clouds, now darting out his rays with dazzling effulgence to create picturesque and magical effects of light and shade; the manifold and beautiful optical effects; the ever-changing nature of the scene; the smiling prospect of distant grove and fertile vale, watered by rivers and dotted with hamlets, villages, and townlets; the clusters of onlookers, who, in their many and various groups, still take up no more than a very little space in all the endless plain – all these things enhance the enjoyment of this best of sports. Add to this that one may, while hawking, enjoy the pleasures of conversation and vary the waiting time by any other amusement that takes one's fancy; and that ladies may take part, either on horseback if they wish to follow the flights, or merely watching the spectacle from some nearby hill or mound. Heron-hawking, though it can often be a rough sort of work, is nevertheless not in the least risky, even for ladies taking part, as long as the horses ridden are used to the country, that reasonable caution is shown when following the flight, and that the participant is willing to fling away the ambition of being always at the head of the field, for it is usual to award that member of the party who gets up to the heron first the privilege of plucking the beautiful black plumes of the nape, which are fixed in the cap as an aigrette, and are the distinctive badge of the falconer.

The field required if heron-hawking is to be carried on every day for two months must contain at least two teams of falconers. Each team consists of four men: a master-falconer and three assistants, of whom one helps the falconer, while the other two take it in turns to do duty as lookout and cadge-boy. All, with the exception of the cadge-boy, must be decently mounted, which makes the number of horses required for the falconers' use six. The number of falcons in each team, when flying daily, must be not fewer than twenty, and not more than twenty-five, bearing in mind that a man cannot manage more than four birds. Assuming, on average, that 7-8,000 1b of butcher's meat (beef of the best quality) and 1200 to 1500 pigeons will be needed to feed 45 falcons for one year, than it will not be difficult to work out the expense that the upkeep of such a team will necessitate if we desire to enjoy the sport in the way just described.

As was noted earlier, only the large falcons can be used for heron-hawking; the tiercel peregrine and the eyass peregrine are not strong

Two scenes of flights at heron were drawn in June-July 1843 by J. B. Sonderland at Loo, in Holland, and represent the activities of the Anglo-Dutch Loo Society for Falconry. The first view shows the moment when the passage heron was seen and at the cry 'A la vol', the party mounted to follow the heron's flight. The second shows the heron flown at brought to the ground, with one falconer making in to it which the other brings the second falcon in to the lure.

Heron gave the most spectacular flights in falconry. If conditions were right, the falconer flew his bird at a heron on passage. The heron would take to the air to escape, ringing up higher and higher, while the falcon endeavoured to climb to position above the quarry in order to put in its stoop. Painting by François Despartes.

enough. The number of falcons to get lost, one after another, when heron-hawking, is quite considerable, amounting to between ten and fifteen birds each season.

Kite-hawking is no whit inferior to heron-hawking in the beauty of the spectacle it affords. To do it successfully, only large falcons, again, can be used – that is, the white and Iceland falcons, the gyr and the saker. The sakret will not do. As kites are nowhere found in large numbers, six or eight falcons will suffice for kite-hawking, which is carried on as follows. Riding out to the locality where kites have been seen, the surrounding fields should be ranged over until one is spied. As soon as this occurs, a tame eagle-owl is released, to whose feet a fox's brush is tied, partly to keep the bird from flying away, and partly to give it a more grotesque appearance. The kite, alerted by the sudden appearance on the scene of one his natural foes, swoops down, if he is soaring, and comes in to the attack. While he is preoccupied with pursuing the owl, the falconers await the moment to cast the falcons. The kite, knowing he will not be able to fight off their attack, decides to escape their clutches by means of the strong wings nature has given him, and soars up into the air in wide rings. The falcons are often forced to follow him up to a vast height before they can work into a position from which to attack, and to repeat their stoops time after time, the kite shifting from the stoops very skilfully, so that there is plenty of interest and excitement for the hawking-party watching the chase. Buzzard and harrier-hawking is carried out in almost the same way as kite-hawking, but was never very common, and is now never practised.

Magpie-hawking, although far less impressive as a spectacle than heron and kite-hawking, is still one the most amusing forms of the sport, largely by reason of the cunning tricks got up to by the magpie in order to escape his attackers, but also by reason of its long duration. Eyass peregrines trained to wait on are usually used for this sport, but passage peregrines may also be used. Flat, open country is the best for this kind of hawking, with a certain amount of low cover in the form of bushes, scattered shrubs, hedges, and so on. For magpie-hawking, a field of two or three falcons and two falconers, preferably mounted, with four or five assistants, or boys, would be required. They should get as near as possible to the place where magpies have been seen before a falcon is cast at one. At the sight of the falcon, the magpie chosen will plunge as fast as she can into the available cover. As soon as they can get up, the falconers and their helpers must be on the spot to flush and chivvy the quarry out of cover; and when it gets up again, the second falcon is cast, and flies at once to the aid of the first. Making sudden, rapid twists and turns with the aid of its tail, the magpie will craftily evade the stoops of its pursuers, and as often as not will succeed in reaching further cover in the shape of nearby bushes or a hedge – or, if not there, will even try to put into a hole or a cart-rut, or dive under carts or between horses' hooves. Driven out of his refuge again by the busy sticks and whips of the beaters, he will finally, overcome by sheer fatigue, fall prey to the falcons. If, on the other hand, he succeeds in gaining a wood, or some tall trees, his favourite refuge when pursued,

A number of painters produced pictures of falconry scenes. David Tenniers chose to depict the moment when a heron has been brought to ground by a cast of falcons. The heron is defending itself vigourously, while above, a further cast fly at another heron.

then no efforts on the part of the beaters to drive him out again will avail. If he takes cover in a hedge, it may be that the only way to chase him out again is to put two men to ride up, one on each side of the hedge, followed by beaters on foot; for the bird is so clever at disappearing from sight that he will secrete himself in the thickest part of the hedge, and skim back along the ground the moment the beaters have passed him by.

For flying at other members of the crow tribe it is possible to use eyass peregrines, or passage birds of either sex. Crow-hawking is an amusing pastime, a kind of by-event on the way to the field, or – if other quarry fails – while actually hawking. For preference, open country should be chosen for crow-hawking. As soon as a crow has been sighted, the falconer tries to approach without frightening it away, not casting the falcon at it until it takes wing, provided that the intervening distance is not greater than a couple of hundred yards. The crow, finding it impossible to escape into cover, will seek safety in flight, either mounting up, or making for some place he can use as a refuge; but, relentlessly pursued by the falcons, he will eventually use up his strength and succumb to their combined attacks. However, if he should succeed in putting into the cover of a bush or a thicket, he must be driven out again by shouting and using those methods described above for the magpie.

Partridge-hawking may be practised with either eyass peregrines, or a goshawk or sparrowhawk; the dedicated falconer will only use falcons; but those whose aim is to catch a large quantity of game will choose the short-wings. When using long-wings, it is usual to ride out to the fields with a pointer and a couple of assistants. The dog, having pointed the partridge, is left on the point, and the falcon is sent up to wait on. If she is well-trained she will climb up to a certain height, but not rake away further than two hundred yards or so. If she does, she must be called to or shown

Another of Fromentin's paintings of nineteenth-century falconry in Algeria. The falcon is taking its pleasure of the quarry.

Thanks to the progress in photography, some astonishing action pictures showing falcons at work have been taken. Left: A saker binds to a pigeon. Below: A peregrine trusses a pigeon. Right: A goshawk with a pigeon as quarry.

the lure, an expedient which must be used with caution in case she gets into the habit of flying too low. Once she is served with a bird, the falcon will stoop at it at once, while the partridge, seeing his deadly foe above, will fly off in the direction of a clump of heather, a copse, or any other cover, provided it is near enough to put into before the falcon has thrown up and returned to the attack. The dog must then be sent in again to flush the partridge out. When the falcon has brought down her bird, the falconer should make in to her carefully and make sure she does not carry the prey; she should be given a few bechins of fresh-killed pigeon, and then taken on the fist and hooded. It is a known fact that partridge will not lie to a dog's point during the latter half of the season, and if that should be the

A rook tries hard to climb above the falcon, or at least to dodge its stoops until it can put in to cover. These birds are often a match for a peregrine.

case, partridge-hawking should be done on horseback, the falcon unhooded on the fist, ready to be slipped the instant the bird gets up. It is also possible to use a line of beaters, ranged fifty or sixty paces apart, in a place where partridge are known to be. The falcon waits on, the falconer remains in the centre of the line in order to control the bird, and the beaters gallop up the line of the beat. However it is managed, a single falcon should take five or six partridge in a day, as long as she is given only a few bechins each time she is flown. When she has made her final kill, she should be given a gorge. When using the goshawk, the matter is managed in the following way. The falconer should keep close to the pointer, and slip the hawk the moment the partridge get up. Not being fast enough to

The aerial ballet of life and death between rook and peregrine. The rook will have to be experienced and alert to dodge the attack.

A pheasant, having been put up by the falconer, heads for cover as fast as possible, with the falcon endeavouring to position to strike.

Right: A peregrine stooping on a cock pheasant. The speed of the falcon's dive may well knock the pheasant out of the air, but once on the ground, a strong cock is a redoubtable opponent.

catch them, she will take stand in a tree or some similar point nearby, and this is done until the hawk manages to kill a partridge. Hunting a goshawk was formerly a popular sport among gentlemen residing in the country, and among people whose means did not allow them to keep falcons. It is, indeed, a pursuit more useful than sporting; it requires little skill and little expense, as it can be carried on on foot and over farmland, and it may be enjoyed by all sorts of people, though true falconers make little of it. The goshawk has not the same powers of flight as the falcon, especially in a wind; and then again it often happens that, when there is a heavy dew, the dogs do all the work, the quarry being so wet that it cannot get up. A sparrowhawk may also be used for partridge-hawking in exactly the same way as a goshawk, and with the identical drawbacks. To be assured of success, young partridge should be pursued, as at this stage they are less fast on the wing than the older birds.

A partnership between man, bird, and dog. These pointers mark grouse on the Scottish moors for the falconers and their peregrines. When the falcon is loosed, the dogs are sent in to flush the grouse, and if all goes well, the peregrine brings its quarry to ground and starts to plume it.

126

For pheasant-hawking, either peregrines or goshawks may be used; the latter might even have the preference, the pheasant being a bird of the woodland, where the hawk is more at home than the falcon. Pheasant will usually lie to the point better than partridge, so it is easier to get up to them, and consequently the goshawk will sometimes catch one at the first attempt, as soon as the pheasant is flushed.

For hares, only the large falcons can be used, that is, the white and Iceland falcons and the gyr. Hare-hawking is best practised in open country, on horseback. Once the dogs have put up a hare, either a single hawk, or a cast, is released, and in repeated stoops will either kill it outright, or stun it, or wound it and so slow it up, or simply in the end wear it out so that the dogs can catch it. Rabbit-hawking is carried on in the same way, and for rabbits, too, the goshawk may be used.

For duck and waterfowl it is usual to use eyass peregrines sent up to wait on. There are, however, a good many disadvantages to the sport, for

Right: A peregrine falcon binding to a partridge. On one side, the fierce joy of the victor, on the other, the despair of the vanquished.

Below: A saker falcon coming in to the lure, showing its long wings and wide spread deck feathers.

A splendid series of action photographs showing a trained eagle in flight. The eagle, king of the birds of prey, was once thought of as a suitable bird for an Emperor to use for falconry. In practice, though, eagles are rarely used, for they can be dangerous, and they are extremely heavy to carry!

it must take place in the vicinity of water, and this gives rise to innumerable difficulties. It is not much practised these days. The same may be said of bustard and stork-hawking, such birds being seldom or never found in the west of Europe.

These notes on the principal forms of hawking will suffice to give the reader a notion of all the other quarry that may be pursued, including the smaller birds such as quail, corncrake, lark, etc. This form of hawking is, however, rare nowadays, and falconers do not usually train hawks for it except to amuse themselves and pass the time if there is nothing more important on hand. We shall confine ourselves to observing that, if falcons are flown at such small quarry, and if the flights are of long duration, as when flying merlins at larks, the bird should be given a gorge when she has made her kill, so that it is possible to get only one flight per day. But if, on the other hand, a sparrowhawk is flown, then the bag at the end of the day will be rather more considerable.

Below: The falcon flies his eagle from the fist. Using its powerful wings, the bird slowly climbs away. Right: Perched on the falconer's fist, this eagle is reminiscent of the eagle standards of Rome or Buonoparte.

132

يَسْأَلُونَكَ مَاذَآ أُحِلَّ لَهُمْ

قُلْ أُحِلَّ لَكُمُ الطَّيِّبَاتُ

وَمَا عَلَّمْتُم مِّنَ الْجَوَارِحِ

مُكَلِّبِينَ تُعَلِّمُونَهُنَّ مِمَّا

عَلَّمَكُمُ اللَّهُ فَكُلُوا مِمَّآ

أَمْسَكْنَ عَلَيْكُمْ وَاذْكُرُوا

اسْمَ اللَّهِ عَلَيْهِ وَاتَّقُوا اللَّهَ

إِنَّ اللَّهَ سَرِيعُ الْحِسَابِ

صَدَقَ اللَّهُ الْعَظِيمُ

an introduction to Arabian falconry

The history of falconry and the Islamic law governing it

The Bedouin have known how to domesticate birds since early pre-Islamic times and how to train them for their own purposes, making some birds dominate others, pitting the strong and more intelligent ones against the weaker and less intelligent and feeding themselves and their dependents on the game thus obtained. This was not simply a means of getting food, but also a form of recreation and a kind of war in times of peace.

The Arabs thought highly of the chase and of a man who fed on what his own hand had brought down. They considered it a proof of his nobility and self reliance and a sign of his honourable attitude towards the possessions of others. He would also share the game with his neighbours and take pride in doing so.

This is still true of the Bedouin today. Among the Arabs a hunter is renowned for self denial. It is a matter of great prestige among his family and tribe when he sets off on the hunting expedition which he has been eagerly awaiting. His enthusiasm for the hunt is apparent to all. His return with the game he has caught gives him the opportunity to manifest his self-denial.

It cannot be said that falconry was the preserve of the opulent and upper classes. Nor was it restricted to the needy and poor. On the contrary, it was open to all and hunting on both land and sea provided recreation and taught the patience, endurance and stealth required on the battlefield. Arab Kings took pride in hunting and eating game and the Arabs were the first to train falcons for hunting purposes. Scholars are agreed in their writings about the hunt that the first man to train falcons for the purpose was Al Harith bin Mu'awiyah bin Thawr bin Kindah.

The story goes that one day while he was watching a man laying a net to snare birds a falcon suddenly alighted on a bird caught in the net and began to devour it. It was not long before a wing of the falcon itself became entangled. Seeing this Al Harith marvelled at it and ordered that the falcon be brought to him and kept in his house, at the same time appointing a keeper to feed and train it for hunting. He used to carry the falcon on his

A page from the Koran, relating to falconry: They ask you what has been made lawful for them. Say: Those things which are good are made lawful for you, and what you have taught the birds of prey and beasts of chase to hunt by training, teaching them as God has taught you. So eat of what they shall catch for you, and mention the name of God over it, and fear God; verily God is swift in reckoning.

135

arm and one day, while on a journey, it spotted a pigeon, took off from Al-Harith's hand, seized and ate the pigeon. Consequently Al-Harith ordered that the bird be trained further, and while out one day, a rabbit broke cover. The falcon pursued and caught it, filling Al-Harith with admiration for the falcon as a hunter of rabbits as well as birds. It was following this episode that the Arabs first came to know about falconry and it soon became a popular sport with them.

With the arrival of Islam with its message encompassing all aspects of life and beliefs, the Arabs began re-shaping their lives on the basis of Islamic tenets and teachings. They took to judging, in the light of the Shari'ah (the Moslem Law), what to retain and what to reject from their

Arab hunting parties in the desert have always taken great care of their falcons, even nowadays pitching a special, ventilated tent for their birds.

Right: For this young Arab boy, the falcon is part of his daily life. He has been brought up with them since he could walk.

136

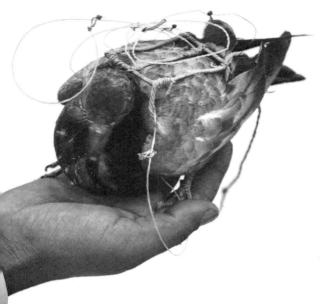

The Arabs use, among other methods, a live pigeon covered with nylon nooses to capture falcons. The bird is tied out, and when the falcon attacks it, it catches its feet in the nooses, and is unable to fly away.

pre-Islamic way of life. It is not surprising therefore, that they should have asked the Prophet – on whom be God's blessings – what, in Islamic terms, was acceptable and what was not permissible in hunting. They had come to fear that which was pre-Islamic because it might be in conflict with Islamic laws. It is related that Zeid al Khabr and 'Adi bin Hatim' asked the Prophet – on whom be God's blessings – about it... 'We hunt with dogs and falcons, but God Almighty has forbidden us to eat carrion.'

At this point, the Quranic revelation came down! 'They ask you what is lawful to them. Say all good things are lawful to you as well as that which you have taught the birds and beasts of prey to catch, training them as Allah has taught you; eat of what they catch for you pronouncing upon it the name of Allah. And have fear of Allah... swift is Allah's reckoning.'

As a result of the revelations of the noble Koran and the great Prophet's traditions, and later interpretations and legal opinions, there emerged a comprehensive law governing all aspects of the hunt. It dealt with animals that exist by hunting and laid down which of them may be

eaten and which many not and stresses the need to cook their flesh. It also rules on the hunter's use of birds of prey and other ramifications covering the entire practice of hunting whether with predatory birds, or, indeed by any other means or weapon, in a way that illustrated the great precision and comprehensiveness of Islamic law and practice.

Game caught by predatory birds is eaten only if taken by a trained bird or animal in a accordance with the Koranic requirement... 'and what ye have taught the birds and beasts of prey', in which the reference is to teaching or training them to hunt. Birds of prey qualify as being 'trained' by their obedience to the hunter's command.

As regard the animals hunted, it is forbidden to eat some of them and permissible to eat others. Thus all birds that have talons with which they kill other animals, such as hawks, falcons, eagles or vultures, are animals which it is forbidden to eat. But animals such as pigeon, which do not hunt or kill, may be consumed.

Game that falls to the huntsman alive must be slaughtered. It is forbidden to eat it if it dies before it is slaughtered and the best 'charity' (Zakat) is to follow the word of God's Prophet – on whom be blessings and peace – 'When ye kill, kill in a seemly manner, and when ye slaughter, slaughter in a seemly manner, and let one of you hone his blade and dispatch the victim without subjecting it to undue suffering.' The hunter himself must say 'In the Name of God' when releasing his falcon. If he deliberately neglects to do so any game caught is not legitimate food. These then, are some of the rules governing hunting according to Islamic Law.

It is customary to share out the meat from the kill among friends and family after it has been cooked. Hunters take pride in this and prominent Arab poets, such as Umrul' Qais and Abu Najm al Ajali and Ash Shamurdal, referred to it in their poems with great pride. Well-to-do people were accustomed to send each other morsels of meat from the kill. It was the significance, rather than material value, that counted.

Another tradition is to choose overcast skies to hunt under because the prey is then at its best and the sport consequently enhanced. On such days it goes in search of good pasture and presents opportunities for sport to the hunter and hunting animals. Such days were particularly favoured by kings. One tradition exclusive to the Moslem hunter was to take only light food and water before setting out to hunt, so that he could actively participate in the chase.

Hunting in the Ommayad Era

We have already considered the importance attributed by the Arabs to hunting in the Jahiliya (pre-Islamic) era and the extent of their attachment to it. The Ommayad era was one in which Moslems enjoyed life, had power over a wide territory and exercised hegemony over a great kingdom. One of the most famous of the Ommayads in his love of hunting, and noted for his domestication of birds of prey, was Yazid bin Mu'awiyah.

Abu al Hassan bin Ali al-Saudi said: 'Yazid loved music, birds of prey, dogs and lynx, and was an enthusiastic hunter, a sport in which he

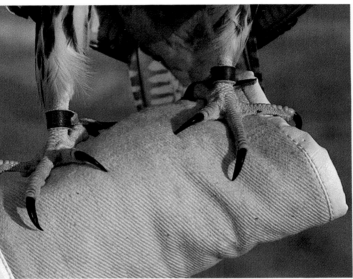

Top: Two views of the 'Hur' falcon, showing the dark eyes and typical falcon beak. In the west, it is known as a saker. Above: The Arabian falconer's sleeve, known as 'Al Menjil'. Below: The padded top of the moveable block, or 'Al Wakr'. Right: All the equipment together.

excelled. He was the first man to have the lynx carried on horseback.' And no wonder, for people in the age of the Ommayads were still close to the life of the desert where hunting and stalking are among the best aspects of life. Nevertheless not all hunters in the days of the Ommayads hunted for pleasure and amusement. There were those among them who took it up in renunciation of worldly riches to live a life of abstinence.

For hunting can be undertaken by two men of different social standing – a king of great wealth and an ascetic of meagre worldly possessions. A king hunts out of love for victory and excitement with all the trappings and pomp. The ascetic hunts in order to escape from the shame of acquiring material profit and to resist the baser instinct of love of possessions and to avoid temptation.

The *Book of Birds* says... 'it was natural that the keeping of birds of prey and hunting birds should not be restricted to the Caliphs but that people in all walks of life should be able to do so as well.' From the evidence collected we find that the keeping of birds of prey, the enjoyment of hunting with them, the expense of keeping them, the use of scientific methods in training them to hunt and the care of their health, were an important part of life in the age of the Ommayads, and that the later Caliphs of this dynasty gave a place in the affairs of the State to hunting and birds of prey.

Hunting in the Abbassid Era

When the Ommayad dynasty came to an end and the Abbassids rose to power, the flag of Islam was flying over some of the most prosperous areas of the world. Taxes gathered from this vast territory poured into the coffers of the Abbassids. The world appeared to be a good and happy place and expectations ran high. Hunting was the favourite sport. One factor which gave the sport an appeal was the Persian influence on the Abbassids. The Persians attached great importance to hunting, achieving fame in the taming and training of birds of prey, expertise in hunting techniques and the production of equipment for it. When they were appointed to positions of influence in the new Abbassid order they brought their knowledge of hunting with them.

The rule of As-Saffah also contributed to the increase in the popularity of hunting among the people. Prior to succeeding to the Caliphate he had spent most of his time hunting, having learned as a small boy and indulged in it in his adolescence, and even as an ageing caliph. As-Saffah was very fond of birds of prey and loved hunting. When his birds failed to make a kill, or did not perform as they should, he would become disheartened, leaving his guards behind and going to hunt with a few intimate friends, such as Khalid bin Safwan. He was very keen on large hunting parties on which relatives and members of his family, his uncles and brother, Mansour, and members of the Court would accompany him. Such expeditions would last several days.

All the Kings of the neighbouring countries knew of Al Mahdi's fondness of birds of prey and his passion for hunting. Michel de Lyon, a great

The falcon, disturbed by the photographer and impatient to fly, bates off the falconer's wrist, but is brought up by the jesses.

140

Left: This young falconer is practising hooding his falcon. Below: A falcon wearing the hood made for it by its falconer. Bottom: This falcon has left its perch, and is standing on the sand at the full length of its leash. Note the large swivel joining the jesses and the leash. Right: One of the Emir of Qatar's falconers, weaving traditional headgear, known as the *koffiye*. The Arabs use a protective sleeve, the *manjalat*, rather than the glove worn in the West.

Byzantine, represented a book on the art of falconry to Al Mahdi written by a prominent writer.

Al Rashid was likewise fond of hunting and reputedly lucky in its pursuit. When so inspired he would show great horsemanship galloping and reining in during the chase. Whenever he heard of someone who had mastered the art of hunting he would send for him and learn from him. He organised magnificent hunts taking with him his friends, members of his court and poets, among them Abu Nawass. He was wont to converse about the pleasures and expertise of hunting with his companions. Al Rashid, like Al Mahdi, was widely known for his love of hunting and everything relating to it. Taqnour, King of Byzantium, on one occasion presented Al Rashid with twelve falcons and three of his hunting dogs as a gesture of goodwill.

Among the Caliphs Al Mu'tassim was the most ardent hunter and horseman giving over a great deal of his time to these things. His hunting expeditions, lasting several days, rejuvenated him physically and uplifted his spirit. The land on which he later built Sammara was chosen by him in the course of a hunting trip. Al Mu'tassim was courageous and self confident, a keen hunter, who would spend half the night discussing the subject with others.

Al Mutawakil, who succeeded to the Caliphate, was no less ardent in his love of hunting than his father although he did not match him in horsemanship or courage. His preference was for hunting with the eagle, a bird of prey which is difficult to capture because it lives in the high mountain peaks, and which is hard to train once it has become mature. Hence its rarity and value among hunters.

The extent of Al Mu'tassim's interest in hunting can best be illustrated by the amounts of money allocated for it in the State budget as compared to other expenditure. During the first years of his reign it ran to 2,500,000 dinars per annum while a daily expenditure of 7,000 dinars was budgeted for the various other aspects of the State's administration of which the following are but a few – The Court, State Security, the Palace Guard, the Army – including mercenaries – Education, Medical Services, Public Works, Religious Affairs, Commissariat, Livestock, Charities, Entertainment, the Civil Service, Artisans, Scholars, and Poets and Prisons.

Seventy dinars were paid daily to those concerned with hunting such as trainers, falconers, etc. Thus one per cent of the total daily budget was set aside for this sport – a clear indication of the degree of importance which Abbassid society attached to the sport of hunting.

Hunting and training in the United Arab Emirates

Throughout ancient times and up to the present, the people of Abu Dhabi have excelled in the training and taming of the falcon and have been ethical in their conduct towards it. This is a heritage passed on from generation to generation. They have developed their own technique of training which is considered to be the best by fanciers and enthusiasts of this sport throughout world.

This technique, which depends on patience, great experience and precision transforms this predator into a gentle, well behaved bird that responds to the orders of its trainer and executes them readily. In this chapter we shall discuss techniques covering the training of 'Al-Hur' (Saker falcon) and 'Ash-Shaheen' (Peregrine), the two birds which the people of this region favour for training and hunting. I have attempted to explain these techniques in a simple and uncomplicated way for the benefit of those who wish to learn about this sport and to appreciate the difference between this method and others, should they have precious knowledge of this noble sport.

Under normal training conditions, the trainer works with one 'Hur' or 'Shaheen' during a season, though an experienced and skiful trainer is capable of training two birds at the same time. It is an accepted fact that the 'Hur' or the 'Shaheen' both need a period of between 30 to 40 days before recognising their owner by his voice or responding to his commands on the hunt, by which time the bird has become tame and disciplined.

At the outset of the training period, the trainer, in domesticating the predator covers its eyes to avoid upsetting it by the unfamiliar sight of the human being. He does this by either using the hood to cover the face or by stitching the eye lids.

The trainer then begins by offering the bird food while talking to it gently and stroking it. The bird continues to feed from the hand of the

Arab falconers, after a day's sport, gathered round the fire in their desert camp. They will drink coffee, dance and sing until late at night.

145

Right: The Arabs call this species of falcon the *shahine*.

Left and below: This falconer has adopted the Western fashion, and wears a falconer's glove. He has just fastened his falcon to the *wekr*, or block.

trainer, hearing his voice and feeling his hands without seeing him until it becomes calm and gains confidence in him. Throughout this period it is carried on the gauntlet so that it gets used to it. After feeding, the bird is gently put on the perch to digest its food.

When the trainer feels sure that the bird has got used to him and is no longer frightened or disturbed by his touch and feeds from his hand confidently, he will from time to time remove the hood from its eyes.

The trainer will then begin to take the bird among people to familiarise it with their voices and slowly encourage it to accept them.

During the initial period of training, the trainer must be very alert and as soon as the bird shows signs of fright he must immediately put on the hood to prevent its being disturbed further.

This period continues for about two weeks after which the bird will be familiar with the voice of his trainer as he calls it to feed.

The trainer should notice that the bird turns towards his voice and that it shows pleasure on hearing it even when its eyes are still covered. The trainer must provide the bird with tender meat and give it adequate quantities of food. The bird must feel satisfied at the end of its meals and it must be fed regularly at the end of the daily training session and after having been called by the trainer repeatedly. During the first weeks, the trainer must be careful not to make any gesture that will frighten the falcon, whether it is a 'Hur' or a 'Shaheen'. As the trainer approaches the bird, which is tied to its perch, he will do well to show it that he is carrying some meat while still at a distance of about ten paces. This will make the bird feel that the trainer is coming to feed it. When the trainer is assured that the bird has seen the food in his hand, he must approach the bird directly and, when close enough to the perch, take a small piece of meat and place it on the perch without touching the bird.

Once the bird gets used to this it will not be startled every time it sees a person approaching. It will associate this with food and in this way become familiar with people in general both during the training period and when it is fully trained and taken on hunts. This familiarity with people is important if the bird should stray from its owner and get lost. At such times any person familiar with the nature of this bird will be able to approach it calmly, stroke it and offer it a piece of meat and easily capture it, either returning it to its owner, if he should know him, or else keeping it for himself to hunt with. At times a well trained bird which is very tame and confident may lose its way and be approached by someone who has no meat with him and who has nothing else with which to tempt the bird, not even a lure.

The second stage is when the falcon is allowed to fly short distances on a long string attached to its leg by the falconer and is taken by him, accompanied by a colleague or a friend, into the open. The companion will place the falcon, with the hood over its eyes, on his arm holding one end of the string between his fingers, the other end being tied to the leg of the falcon. The owner moves about fifty metres away and begins calling the falcon by its given name in a loud voice. He will repeat this several times

One of Sheikh Zaid's mounted falconers, a photograph taken by the well-known explorer Wilfred Thesinger.

A modern-style falconry party in the deserts. Land Rovers and such-like vehicles are increasingly used to carry the parties out to the hunting grounds.

while waving the lure in the air. When the person carrying the falcon is certain that it has heard the call by turning its head towards the voice, he will remove the hood and release it from his hand. The bird will fly towards its owner who will give it food while talking to it. This operation should be repeated for several days until the owner is certain that the bird has been taught to come to him from a short distance just by calling to it and waving the lure in the air, and that it is eating its food contentedly, and completely unafraid.

This is followed by the last stage of training which involves calling to the bird from long distances. During this phase, the trainer takes the falcon away from the city into the desert, not forgetting to have with him the gamebag in which he carries all that is needed for training the falcon. The trainer leaves the falcon with a fellow trainer and takes up a position about one kilometre away and proceeds to call to it in a loud voice until the falcon hears him and pays attention to him.

149

Above the falconer, on the right the owner. Together with the falcon, they make up a partnership often found in Arab lands.

Left: Two falconers take a break during a training session. The falcon is perched on the lure, which has been used to exercise it.

While repeatedly calling to it, the trainer also waves the lure never ceasing to call it in the same pitch. The companion removes the hood and releases the bird which darts like an arrow towards its owner, seizing the lure in one quick aggressive swoop. The trainer talks to the bird while he takes the string attached to the lure away from the bird. The bird returns to the attack once more, striking hard at the lure. It then rises a little and swoops down on the imitation bird.

Meanwhile the trainer is talking to the bird which is trying hard to get at the lure, but the falconer teases it without letting it do so, talking to it all the time. The falcon prepares to eat the lure and the trainer will produce pieces of meat from between the feathers of the lure without the falcon noticing, allowing it to eat the meat until it is satisfied. While the falcon is eating, the trainer talks to it, encouraging it to eat. The trainer must allow the falcon to complete its meal from the lure before placing it on the gauntlet thereby making sure that the falcon thinks it is eating the flesh of a real bird and not that of the lure. The trainer must bring the meat out from between the wings of the lure and, holding it by the tips of his fingers, while still keeping it covered by the wing feathers, allow the bird to eat some of the feathers with the meat. This is advisable for two reasons. The first is that it is good for the falcon while in training to eat a small live bird and the other is that the small amount of feathers it eats is useful for cleaning out its stomach. In about seven hours after feeding, the falcon will excrete the feathers along with all other waste material it has eaten.

151

The falconer must examine the excreted feathers very carefully and if he finds any remnants it means that the falcon is not digesting its food well. He must then miss a feed. If this condition persists, the falconer must treat the bird until the droppings are dry and not loose, indicating that the stomach of the falcon has recovered and the digestive system is working normally.

It is not necessary for the falcon to eat feathers regularly, but only at certain intervals, otherwise it will become sick and its treatment take a long time.

When the falcon begins to feed off the lure greedily, the trainer must put the hood on its eyes and place it carefully on the gauntlet, allowing it to digest its food. This exercise must be done twice a day, in the early morning and in the evening.

When the falcon is tamed it will be a trained and disciplined bird and its master can confidently take it on a hunt. There are a number of things that the falconer or hunter must have at hand while on a hunt. He must have pieces of meat in his gamebag, as well as a few live pigeons and a long piece of string and the lure, which must always be with him. The lure is very important during the hunt. It can happen that the falconer releases his falcon to hunt down a prey which is aware of the falcon and will dart away. If the prey is a strong flier, it will travel far and the falcon will try to catch up with it, flying into the distance, away from the falconer. The falcon might lose its sense of direction and not return to its waiting master. The falconer will follow in the general direction of the falcon's flight, searching for the bird between the desert shrubs. He might come upon the falcon to find it has succeeded in making a kill and has fed on its prey. He will approach it slowly, before it has finished feeding. In such instances the falconer will use the lure which he has in his gamebag by throwing it into the air and holding on to one end of the line to which it is tied. He will also speak in a loud voice to the falcon which will hear its masters and turn towards his voice, and, seeing the lure, drop its prey and follow the lure, striking at it and catching it. In the meantime, the falconer is still speaking to his bird while drawing the string gently towards him until the falcon is within arms reach. He will then capture the bird, cover its eyes with the hood and return it to the gauntlet while speaking to it gently until it regains its confidence in its master.

Other unexpected events may occur on a hunt. The falconer may have launched the falcon after a strong-flying bird and while in the air the falcon might see a large predator, like an eagle, of which it is afraid. The falcon will let go of its prey and fly rapidly away from the eagle, losing its way going far from its owner, and not return. As in the previous example, the falconer will go in the direction of the disappearing falcon and call it in a loud voice, throwing up the lure. He will also take a live pigeon and tie the end of the leash to which it is secured to the stump of a bush. The search is therefore made by calling to the bird in a loud voice, and by using the lure and the live pigeon. The falconer will remain in the same place even after nightfall and will sleep there, until dawn when he begins calling to the falcon again. Very often the lost falcon may have tired from flying and hunting and will rest in the shade of a bush. It might not have seen the lure or live pigeon but it may have heard the voice of its trainer from afar, being a fully trained falcon. It will come to its master who will quickly offer it some food – not less than one 'dirham' of tender flesh – since the falcon has learned to respond to the call to food from the start of its training.

All well trained falcons hunt, but there is a difference in how each falcon attacks its prey. Some falcons truss their prey in the air and excel in their flying and circling manoeuvres tiring their prey in the air and finding the right opportunity for the attack. Other falcons prefer to launch their attack by striking while their prey lies on the ground by devious manoeuvres which intimidate and demoralise the prey, then pouncing for the kill. Other falcons are afraid of attacking the prey when it is on the ground. This is especially true when hunting for bustard. This is because the falcon is reluctant to bite at the strong legs of the bustard and is afraid of the sticky substance known by people of the desert as 'tamal', which is emitted by the bustard when attacked. Each falcon differs from the others in its ability and potential and a trainer must be able to assess these qualities in his falcon in order to get the best out of it in the hunt without over-exerting it and making it too tired to hunt.

Training does not merely mean teaching the bird of prey how to hunt, how to launch it after the prey, and come back with it. It has other aspects which the skilful trainer must be aware of to help his falcon in hunting its prey. He must be knowledgeable about the variety of birds which his falcon is most adept at hunting and familiar with their habitats and the tactics they adopt to hide from the falcon. Falconers in the Gulf area have sufficient experience to track down the birds and determine whether the tracks are old or recent enough to indicate that they are still somewhere in the area.

The evidence of the existence of the birds to be hunted, whether bustard or plover, is footmarks in the sand. If they are clearly detailed and not blurred, it means that they are recent. If they are depressed and blurred by the wind, they are old. However, it is not possible to rely on this if winds have been blowing in the area for some time. Under such circumstances other evidence must be looked for to determine the existence of wild birds in the area in which the falconer is searching. One is the droppings of the birds which, if solid and dry, must have been there for a long time, but if soft and loose is recent. The falconer helps the falcon not to over exert itself in the search for a bird of prey and not to show itself to its would-be victims as they do in the West.

A good trainer will, on the contrary, know when to remove the hood to conserve the bird's strength for the hunt, saving its energy for a number of successful attacks. If the hunting ground is on an elevation that overlooks an open plain the falconer can depend on the falcon to search for its bird of prey. This is especially true if the prey is clearly defined against the horizon and within three metres range of the sharp-eyed falcon. At times wild birds and small animals hide themselves in areas which are far from the birds of prey, each having its own hiding place, either in the ground or among the shrubs and weeds.

This is especially true of the bustard, plover and rabbits. In such instances the falcon is unable to discover their hiding places even if only a few metres away from it. The falconer uses his experience to assist the falcon in discovering the hiding places of the birds and directs it towards them. This needs patience and effort and close observation because evidence of the existence of these can only be seen at close range.

The falconer must care for the cleanliness of his falcon by cleaning its feathers of dirt and thorns and keeping its beak clean at all times, removing all remnants of flesh after feeds.

The talons and feet of the falcon have also to be cared for, its wings examined closely and its body, colour of the feathers, and the colour and shine of its eyes kept under observation. The falconer must be certain that the wings and feathers are in a healthy condition.

Right: A saker, or 'Hur' bates off from the gauntlet. The falconer was aged 91 when the photograph was taken.

Below: A Peregrine mantles over its prey, which it is engaged in pluming, or removing the feathers before breaking in to feed on it.

Hunting and capturing the Falcon

There are several ways of hunting the falcon, not differing greatly from each other but all having the same objective.

1 *The Cave Method*

The hunter goes out early in the morning with an assistant to search for falcons by following their trail. This consists of clear traces made by the falcon's talons in the sand and by remains of its food found around rocks or stones in the desert. Other signs of its presence in the vicinity are pieces of regurgitated food dropped from its mouth on stones or the sand. Once the hunter is certain that falcons are in the area he prepares his strategy for hunting them.

He starts by preparing a deep hole in the ground, big enough for him to stand in without any part of his body showing above the ground and wide enough for him to sit in if the waiting period is prolonged. He keeps some food and water with him in the hole.

Once the hole is ready the hunter releases a pigeon tied to a long string. A falcon will see the pigeon, hunt it down and begin to eat it. The hunter and his assistant then approach the falcon, which leaves its prey and flies away. The hunter hides in the hole, holding on to the string which is tied to the pigeon while his assistant covers the hole with tree branches and weeds and then himself hides at a distance from the hole. Once the falcon feels no one is present it returns to the pigeon to feed on it again. The hunter pulls very carefully and slowly on the string so as not to disturb the falcon until it is within his reach. He catches it by the legs, above the claws, with his hand extended from a small opening in the cover of the hole. He places the falcon in the 'Qifa', a piece of cloth made specially to hold the captured bird and protect the hunter. The hunter closes the eyes of the falcon by pulling a thread over the eyelids, calms it down, then puts a jess on its legs and gives it over to his trainers.

2 *The Netting Method*

This is a modern method in which the hunter ties the legs of a pigeon and places it in a strong net knotted in a gauge of a size designed to entrap the falcon's claws.

After satisfying himself of the presence of falcons in the vicinity he releases the pigeon into the air. The falcon hunts it down and feeds on it and, its talons becoming snared in the net, is unable to escape.

Training equipment

1 *The Gamebag*

This is a bag made of white straw or very often cotton, with an adjustable strap of the same material. The strap can be shortened or lengthened by threading it through a fixed loop and then knotting it. As the falconer usually carries live pigeons in the bag, he shortens it to fit snugly under his arm when slung across his shoulder, to prevent the pigeons from escaping while he is busy hunting. The shorter the strap the less the falconer is encumbered by the extra weight during his movements. Besides pigeons the gamebag contains pieces of tender meat, a long thread and a sharp knife. The knife is for the falconer to dispatch, without delay, the game hunted down by the falcon, according to accepted practice. The gamebag also holds the falconer's simple personal effects.

This resembles a pair of spectacles, the size of the bird's head, with a small opening in the middle for the beak. It is made of soft leather, painted and decorated by the maker. The falconer places it over the head of the bird by holding it from its crest and then tightening the leather laces around the bottom of the hood. It is then made firm by pulling a thread on either side and putting the laces through the same openings but in the opposite direction. This allows the falconer to control the hood which is very gently and carefully placed on the bird's head while talking and stroking it continuously, especially if the falcon shows signs of being uneasy or frightened. After making certain that the patch is correctly in place, the falconer and one of his colleagues, or a trainer, tightens the laces from either side while carrying the falcon on his arm. If no one is at hand to help him, the falconer uses his teeth to tighten one lace and his hand for the other.

2 The Hood ('Al Burqa')

This protects the falconer from the talons of the falcon and is always carried on his hand. Made of thick material, it is filled with straw or a softer substance and covered on the outside with velvet. The two openings are lined with soft leather or thin plastic. Its thickness protects the arm of the falconer, yet it is flexible so as not to injure the falcon's talons. The falconer wears it just above his wrist with his fingers free to feed the bird while it sits on his arm.

3 The Hand Shield or Gauntlet ('Al Menjil')

A thick coloured thread or rope, sometimes made of soft plastic, plaited and strong. The leash is 30 cms long and divided into two equal parts. One end is tied to the legs of the bird and the other end to the jess (or 'mursil') which is attached to the perch or the gauntlet.

The leash is secured to the legs of the falcon and when it has caught its prey the trainer can approach it quietly while the falcon is busy feeding on it and tie the leash to the jess which is fixed on to the gauntlet. This enables the falconer to carry the bird off after it has finished eating and restricts it from flying beyond the reach of the falconer.

4 The Leash ('As-Sabbug')

This compliments the other equipment used in controlling the movements of the bird and preventing it from escaping. It is a rope, a little thicker than the leash, 120 cms long in three sections divided by a metal ring with a swivel which revolves (on a 180 degrees axis) in all directions. The nut joining the two sections of the rope, allows the falcon to move in any direction and to get off its perch, or the falconer's arm, without injury.

Being able to jump on or off its perch gives the bird freedom of movement and an impression of not being restricted. The third section of the jess is attached to the perch permanently. Once the falconer has finished working with the falcon, he covers its face with the hood and ties the attached end of the jess to the falcon's leg, leaving it to digest its food quietly.

5 The Jess ('Al Mursil')

The falcon perches secured to its perch by the falconer for resting and sleeping. The perch is a metal peg covered in the middle with decorated wood. The top of the perch is circular, filled with soft cotton, and covered on the outside with velvet or soft leather to enable the falcon to stand comfortably withart damage to its feet.

The perch can be readily implanted in the ground and stabilised to prevent the falcon falling off. Its height varies, depending on the falconer's preference, the size of the falcon and the nature of the ground.

After many years experience in experimenting with and training falcons and hunting with them,my preference is for 'Al-Hur'. This is essentially because it is a patient hunter with greater strength and power in the chase than the Shaheen. It is also faster over long distances and more capable of making a kill. Some people maintain that 'Al-Hur' has inferior breathing capacity, but my personal experience with the species does not support this. The most significant feature of 'Al-Hur' is that it is always ready for hunting, having moulted and grown new feathers a few weeks before the hunting season begins or just before its commencement.

This is an important attribute because it permits the hunter to take full advantage of the hunting season. The natural habitat of 'Al-Hur' is the desert which provides the rabbits, mice and wild birds on which it feeds.

'Al-Hur' has great fortitude and puts up with hunger and harsh conditions, accepting whatever food is at hand. It is contented by nature, is calmer and less sensitive than other predators, taking better to domestication although it is more aggressive in attacking its prey. In flight it is also one of the most stable of predators and the strongest, seizing and overcoming its prey with great determination. The tail of 'Al-Hur' is short. It has powerful flanks, a large head and is dust-coloured with strong yellow legs and beak, sharply curved.

Qualities that make for a good falcon include redness of colour, a wide head, long neck, a broad breast, full throat, wide midriff, robust thighs, short legs, broad wingspan, a medium sized tail, flat feet, heavy claws, a black tongue, a small nose with wide nostrils, and wings which fold scissor-like on its back. These qualities combine to make it a strong, confident and very fast hunter.

The colour of the falcon is either a greyish or pure white, red, or yellow with red or green undertones, or of the black varieties which live only in caves or recesses and on mountain slopes but not in trees or on mountain peaks. The hawk requires little water in winter but more in summer.

The 'Al-Hur' moults as do the eagles and shaheen. When its wings have almost completely moulted its owner will keep it indoors until the process is completed. During the moulting season the falcon needs only to be fed with tender meat, especially that of birds, field mice or rabbits. It should not be fed on the flesh of cows, sheep or the camel regularly and never for more than a week. It requires water as normally.

158

6 *The Perch or Block ('Al Wakr')*

Species of Falcon found in the Arabian Gulf

Al-Hur (Saker falcon)

The Moulting of 'Al-Hur'

Right: The Arabian version of the falcon's block. Since in the desert, trees are few and far between, this practical invention can be stuck in the sand, and the falcon leashed to it. It is known as a 'wakr', Arabic for nest.

The place where the falcon is kept while moulting should always be clean and kept free of insects, fleas and lice etc., and always be well ventilated. If it is comfortable and at ease the bird's new feathers will grow in forty days from the end of the period of moulting. In the hunting field the head of the falcon should be covered with the hood when moulting to prevent it from attacking the falconer without reason or from chasing prey and thereby tiring itself unnecessarily.

'Al-Hur' hunts bustard, rabbit and plover, but never the gazelle. There are various types of the 'Al-Hur' which differ in size, body structure, wingspan, colour and eyes. They are popularly identified in the area by the names of 'al-Jarmoushah' and 'Wukra al-Harrar'.

Wukra al-Harrar

The 'Wukra al-Harrar' is usually a little smaller than 'Al-Hur', though some are similar in size. It requires the same methods for its training and development. They are sometimes very aggressive, at times even more so than 'Al-Hur'. This type is red in colour with yellow undertones and its most distinguishing feature, which is exclusive to it among predators, is its black eyes and red colouring on the top of its head. Its nose and feet are normally yellow. It hunts the same prey as 'Al-Hur', moults in the same way and needs the same kind of nourishment.

Al-Jarmushah

This is smaller than 'Al-Hur' and 'Al-Wukra' and can be red, black, golden or white in colour. Its feet and claws are small, the nostrils small and nose narrow. It is characterised by its patience and courage, qualities which also exist in 'Al-Hur'. It hunts the same prey as 'Al-Hur' and 'Al-Wukra' and moults like them.

Ash-Shaheen (Peregrine Falcon)

The 'Shaheen' is a 'sea' bird of the Hawk species, living close to the coast and feeding on water birds. There is another variety of water bird called 'ad-Duma' which belongs to the eagle species of which more will be said later in this book.

Relatives of the Shaheen falcon are known by the local population as 'Wubra ash-Shaheen' and 'Taba' ash-Shaheen'. Subsequent pages will contain more about this falcon also.

The Arab name 'Shaheen' is derived from the Persian and means 'balance' relating to the fact that this falcon can tolerate neither extreme hunger nor a surfeit of food. The Shaheen falcon is short tempered and angers quickly, especially when aged. Though it responds to training and discipline it must be handled with gentleness and sympathy. It is said to be 'more fragile than glass'. Its tolerance of hardship and fatigue is less than of the hawk and it is smaller in size. It is faster than all the other species when hunting over short distances and the most agile in its movements when in flight. In chasing its prey the Shaheen shows great aptitude and competence, and although very aggressive, its ability is surpassed by that of the hawk over long distances because of its inferior breathing capacity.

Our experience of hunting with the Shaheen is that it will not relinquish its prey on the command of its trainer nor give it up for the lure. One of its short-comings is that it is a late moulter and is only ready for hunting towards the end of the season, for a month or less. This is disadvantageous to a full enjoyment of the hunting season. In most instances when living with its owner over a long period, the Shaheen tends to ignore many aspects of its training and shows a lack of discipline in its behaviour. The Persians are better acquainted with the Shaheen than the Arabs since it is found in large numbers in their country. They are more knowledgeable than others about its conduct, methods of training and how best to hunt with it as they have been doing since ancient times.

Colours of the Shaheen: Totally black: black head and back with a mixture of white on the stomach or yellow and white mottled with golden red extremities. Some have white heads. The favoured variety has a wide head, large sharp eyes, a long neck, thick throat and wide midriff, robust thighs with short legs, long wings, short tail, flat feet and sparse and pliable feathers with a thin tail. It hunts the same varieties of game as the 'Hur'. The same techniques are used in training it except that it takes longer to train than the Hur due to its temperament and slow response.

Wakri Ash Shaheen

In size the Wakri Ash Shaheen is usually similar to the Shaheen but sometimes slightly smaller. In general its colours resemble those of the Shaheen with red head feathers and yellowish eyes. Its shape is also very much like that of the Shaheen but distinguishable by its differing feet, long talons and yellow nostrils. In temperament it is less excitable and easily adaptable to training. It hunts various types of small birds and the rabbit.

Tabe' Ash Shaheen

This is the third of the breeds of Shaheen. It is similar in shape to the other two. By comparison to the Wakri it is inferior in both size and weight with a small head and mouth and fine legs. It, also, is cooler in temperament than the Shaheen. Its plumage is usually spotted, particularly on the breast, with white spots. The Wakri abounds in coastal areas where it feeds on both marine and land birds. It is easier to train than the Shaheen.

The Sparrowhawk

The Sparrowhawk ('Al Bashiq') differs from the Hawk ('Al Baz') in both size and weight. It is tamer and more easily domesticated. Although it is among the smallest of hunting birds it is one of the swiftest in take-off and flight. But it is nervous and sensitive in its disposition. Like the hawk, it is quick tempered and high spirited. It is a particularly handsome bird, attractive in the way it carries itself. In performance it is in the same class as the hawk and hunts pigeons and smaller birds.

The Sparrowhawk is usually small in its overall size of body – a point for which it is greatly favoured although larger examples are not disdained. It is found in red, green and yellow. The red-bodied bird, with a back, is patient and strong in endurance, while that with a red back and

Above: Falcons resting on their blocks after a day's hunting in the desert. The birds expend a great deal of energy in their hunting, and need a quiet and undisturbed sleep if they are to show good sport on the morrow.

abdomen is weaker and impatient. The best quality of sparrow hawks are regarded as those which have been reared since before their first moulting. They are trained for hunting in the same ways as the hawk.

The Goshawk

The goshawk is the bird most resembling a small eagle, but it is not favoured in Abu Dhabi because it does not excel in hunting bustard and plover, although it is excellent for hunting rabbits. In the West this species of predator is popular for hunting woodcock, grouse and pheasants and other wild birds.

162

Hunting techniques in the West differ from those of the Arabs, largely because of the difference in environment and climate. We have large open spaces with plains and valleys, whereas the West is largely forest.

In the Gulf the trainer relies entirely on his own judgement, skill and proficiency and the training of the hawk in hunting down the quarry and in knowing where to find it. When he goes out to hunt bustard, plover or rabbit, the hunter searches for them on his own and tracks them down. The hawk is one of the most skilful predatory hunters, the most noble and the most expensive. It has been contrasted with the falcon and described as being 'the blue bearded bird with the short wing and fine proportions'.

It is an intelligent predator, sensitive and dignified. It is also courageous, fast in the attack and feared by all birds of its size.

The qualities looked for are a small head, a neck as thick as it is long, wide eyes, rounded ears and crop, compact claws, tail, and thighs, slender legs, flat feet, balanced gait, a good eater, continuously biting, strong in flight, quick of understanding and with wide jawbones.

Arab falconers consider the best variety of falcons to be those with sparse feathers, reddened and sharp eyes. The blue eyed red falcon is inferior. Still more inferior is the yellow one. Most inferior of all are those with hard flesh, long tails, short wings, small heads and yellow eyes. The superior falcon is greyish-white in colour.

The falcon has qualities which distinguish it from other predators. It dives and attacks with great speed. Some say that it is faster than the arrow and the speed with which it seizes its prey is proverbial.

Many have testified to the loyalty of the falcon once it has been disciplined and trained to keep its place.

The falcon likes to shelter in areas where trees are high and there is ample shade and water, but will not nest except in thorny trees. It builds a firm nest to protect it from the rain and heat when about to hatch its eggs.

In order to protect the falcon, and because of the special status with which it is regarded by its fanciers, falconers have committed themselves to be governed in their attitude towards it by a set of rules prescribing the ethics of falconry. Under these rules of conduct a person carrying a falcon should have clean clothes on, be clean himself, be of good character and knowledgeable about the falcon. It is also ruled that it should not be carried by an executioner. This would interfere with its zest for hunting and turn it against the person carrying it. If an executioner carries the falcon for three successive days, it will recognise him and evade him whenever he approaches. If it is carried by a pleasantly scented person, a falcon will show contentment and pleasure and perch on his arm confidently. The falcon is a sensitive predator and revolted by all things that upset a gentle creature. With this in mind the rules of conduct admonish the person carrying the falcon not to eat garlic or onions or any other food which leaves an offensive smell on the breath. The falcon is a dignified bird full of pride and will not accept any insult. Trainers are required not to shout at it, or reprimand it, in order not to prejudice good relationships with it and to ensure an atmosphere of companionship.

The Eagle

The eagle is one of the greatest birds of prey and the largest except for the vulture. It has strong claws, feathered legs and copious beak. The bedouin use an irregular plural for the bird's name. The Arabs call the eagle 'Al Kasir' denoting its strength and ability to attack by diving on its prey. The eagle has a fierce, imposing and dignified appearance and inhabits the peaks of craggy mountains.

The eagle is found in many and varied colours. Some are brilliant black in places, some black mottled, others are black and white or varying shades of red. Some carry white spots on the head, others have white legs, while some have yellow and white stripes.

The eagle most favoured is the one reared from youth. The white eagle is not easily tamed. The best are those of dependable character, courage and of the red variety.

The eagle of North Africa has a bolder face than the eagle of the Arab east and is a more powerful hunter. It is one of the most violent birds of prey and the fastest when making a kill. As a bird of prey the eagle is difficult to capture. It has excellent vision, is sharp of hearing, very courageous, light of wing, fast moving and can soar to great heights or swoop earthwards.

One of the characteristics of the eagle is that it rarely hunts for itself, preferring to pillage its food from other birds of prey. It perches on a high vantage point and seeing that a bird of prey has hunted down a victim, it swoops down on it. Fearing the attack by the eagle, the other bird relinquishes its prey to escape. When the eagle is hungry no feathered creature is safe from it, not even the falcon which is also a hunter. It even feeds on snakes, but not their heads.

Despite its regality and great courage the eagle can be tamed by the falconer. If trained it will hunt. If restrained, it will respond. It can be reared in captivity. It is malleable, tame and yet a hunter.

One species of eagle, known as the 'Dammi' (Osprey or Fish-Hawk), hunts its prey in water. When striking its prey it can dive to a depth of over three feet. This 'Water Eagle' dives with its head between its legs, extending its claws forward pointedly, descending at great speed and seizing the fish with its claws then rising from the water with similar speed. It is distinguishable from other birds of prey by the colour of its eyes which, like cats', are blue and sometimes grey. Big and medium sized eagles hunt gazelle, the medium sized being the faster in the attack. The greatest users of the eagle in hunting gazelle are the Syrians and the Moroccans.

Diseases of the Falcon and their treatment

Falcons like all other creatures are subject to diseases, some of which are easily treated, while others are more difficult to cure. When a falcon falls sick it is isolated from the others to avoid contamination. The ancient falconers became experts in the treatment of these diseases by using the traditional cures which the bedouin of the United Arab Emirates continue to employ in treating some of the diseases which afflict their falcons.

However, these ancient methods are currently being supplemented by modern treatments which are becoming known through veterinary specialists who have developed an interest in this aspect of medicine. A number of them have acknowledged the value of the older cures while maintaining that the new medicines are easier to administer and more effective. It is imperative that the falconer be concerned with the health of his bird and though it is not necessary that he should be knowledgable about all the symptoms of the diseases, and the methods of treatment, there are certain indications which can determine the state of health of the falcon. Some important symptoms are that the colour of the beak is clear, that it spreads its wings and that the two thigh bones should be straight and normal in size. Another significant factor in determining the health of a falcon is the excrement which equates with the waste and water excretion of the human body. And just as an efficient doctor can diagnose a disease in the human being by examining stools and urine an observer of birds in general, and of falcons in particular, can diagnose the sickness by studying the colour of the droppings.

If the excrement of the bird is a solid unfragmented mass, of a definite white colour but slightly tinged with black and easily excreted, then the falcon is healthy. Any change in the colour of the excrement signifies that the falcon is not well and the falconer must treat it. If it is white with a little black, is fragmented and coarse and excreted with difficulty, the falcon has indigestion. In cases where the white in the excrement merges with the black, the black is predominant, the falcon is suffering from fatigue. If, in addition, the excrement emerges in rounded rather than elongated segments, the infection is a long standing one. Symptons such as shortness of breath, little appetite for food, loss of weight, nasal congestion, the excrement yellowish, due to the white and black merging, indicates that the falcon has a disease comparable to tuberculosis in a human being. When the falcon refuses its food repeatedly, then it is dyspeptic and the falconer must not feed it other than small pieces of lamb the size of a coffee bean mixed with goat's or camel's milk, leaving the falcon to rest on its perch until it appears normal again. When the falcon twitches its head nervously and shows signs of restlessness if carried, beating its head against its breast, this is an indication that a feather has stuck in its throat or that it is suffering from a lack of breath. When the bird ruffles its feathers, hiding its head behind its wings and lifting its leg under its stomach, keeping its mouth open, breathing continuously and closing its eyes, it has a fever. When a falcon jumps erratically on the arm of its carrier, then the hood covering its eyes is too tight or it has heard a sound which it interprets as calling it to food. If the jumping becomes excessive the falcon probably has lice which cause a severe illness by infecting its feathers and contaminating it, at times permanently damaging the bird. Lice can breed on the body of the bird due to negligence on the part of the falconer when meat is fed to the falcon and small pieces are left in its beak. When going to sleep at night the falcon normally tucks its head under its wings and if remnants of meat are stuck to its beak, lice hatch among the feathers and contaminate the body. Lice on the falcon are not easy to see because they become embedded among the feathers and are yellow in colour. Evidence of lice can be discerned by the restlessness of the bird and its ruffling of its feathers and its extreme weakness. In cases where the bird is infected by smallpox indicated by small red spots on the legs and tip of the nose, the cure is to heat a nail and apply it to the spots. This however, must not be undertaken before the spots have formed scabs and only on those that are on the nose, since those on the legs fall off on their own.

The falconer should not make an immediate judgement on the ailment of the bird based on either the observation of its droppings or other symptoms mentioned above. The change in the condition of the bird's health may be due to having eaten meat which has upset its stomach and the change in the colour of the excrement merely temporary. The falconer therefore has to examine the condition of the bird in detail by observing its eyes, body, feathers, beak, claws and its digestive process before making a judgement on its condition and a diagnosis of its ailment. Having ascertained that the falcon is ill, the falconer must show it sympathy and having established the nature of the disease begin treatment during this time, the bird should be well nourished since it is better to treat a robust bird than a sickly, weak one.

The Bustard

The bustard is one of the wild birds with which the people of the Gulf are very familiar and enjoy hunting with the falcon. In Arabic the same gender is used for the name of the male and female of the species. It is strong in flight and covers great distances. It is grey in colour and both its neck and beak are long.

A significant feature of the bustard is its inbuilt weapon for self defence consisting of a gland lying between its tail-end and stomach for storing a thin but sticky liquid. When attacked by a falcon the bustard manoeuvres against its assailant by circling above and below it, and to the left or right of it, until it finds the opportunity to spray this substance on the falcon. Because its feathers become stuck together the falcon is restricted in its movements and becomes submissive and, if off its guard, is killed by the bustard. The falcon is well aware of the advantage the bustard has over it, and continues the attack from the flanks. Then flying above the bustard, it allows it to release the liquid, which it tries to evade and, if it succeeds, it then attacks the bustard.

The people of the Gulf call this sticky substance 'Tamal' or the abundant spray (marash min al fayidh). They regard the bustard as stupid and say that there is no bird so foolish because it deserts its eggs and sits on those of others. It is characteristic of the bustard to die of melancholy if during the moulting season its new feathers are slow to appear and it is therefore incapable of flying. Other bustards will leave it behind.

The flesh of the bustard is a cross between that of chicken and duck in texture, but more tender than duck.

The bustard includes thirty-two species, twenty-three of which are exclusive to Africa, while the rest inhabit Asia, Europe and Australia.

The body sizes of the different species vary from large to medium but all are strong and robust with thick, medium sized necks and large heads. They have strong beaks which are shorter than the head and conical and arched at the end of the upper section. Their feet are of medium size, strong, with three talons, and their wings are developed and rounded.

The talons are long, the third being longer than the others, and the tails have between sixteen and twenty broad feathers. The feathers on the body are thick and tough and quite often rather long on the head and neck. Bustard are deficient in oil glands. The males of the species are larger than the females and surpass them in the beauty of their feathers while adolescents greatly resemble the female.

A feature of the bustard is the existence of a large pouch underneath the skin of its neck lying alongside the windpipe and ending at the lower part of the tongue where it curves towards the backbone. Only the fully grown males have this pouch which is filled with air during the mating

The falcon and its prey, in this case a MacQueen's Bustard, or 'hubara'.

167

season and deflated at other times when an opening under the tongue becomes evident. Bustard live in open fields and plains but avoid forests. They live in a solitary state or in small groups gathering in large flocks after breeding and settling permanently in the southern regions while those that live in temperate areas are either migratory or transient.

Despite their weight, bustard are quick in their movements, walking on land with a balanced gait that can quickly develop into a run. In flight they can accelerate their speed very quickly. They are by nature cautious and cannot be easily tricked or deceived. They live peaceably with others of their species but are very aggressive when their jealousy is aroused and never hesitate to take on birds as strong or as large as themselves. They feed on seeds, cereals, fruit, the leaves of trees and other greenery. The mating season is at the end of autumn when the bustard pair off. The males, which normally are satisfied with only one female, become restless at this time. They nest in hollows in the wheat fields or between the shrubs and weeds in open country. The female cares for her young without any assistance from the male which returns to guard them. Young bustard develop at a slower rate than other birds and need longer to reach full maturity and become independent of their parents.

A Report on the International Conference on Falconry and Conservation held in Abu Dhabi 10th to 18th December 1976

compiled by Yehya Badr

Why the Conference was held

When His Highness Sheikh Zaid bin Sultan, the President of the United Arab Emirates, issued invitations to the world's first international conference on falconry his decision to do so was influenced by the course of events during a visit he made to Austria in the summer of 1975. By this time his name was already closely connected in the minds of falconers in many parts of the world with the preservation of the sport, which he regards as part of Arabia's ancient heritage. Appropriately carrying their hawks on their wrists, a number of enthusiasts visited His Highness during the course of his stay to exchange views and discuss the many aspects of falconry, particularly methods of training and maintaining their birds. This led to correspondence and suggestions as to how best the sport could be kept alive. News of the visit and subsequent developments soon spread among falconry devotees in Europe and America and the idea of convening a conference at which experts on the subject could meet and discuss it eventually emerged. Many of them accepted His Highness' invitation to hold the conference in the United Arab Emirates.

The objectives of the Conference would be to put forward recommendations for preserving and promoting falconry by providing accurate information about its historical background and its educational and social merits. In anticipation of a wide response preparations for hosting a large number of experts and personalities of world-wide fame in this field were put in hand and invitations sent out. Over two hundred acceptances from interested falconers were received.

A part of the preparations necessitated approaches to museums and libraries with a view to obtaining material on loan which could be

168

German falconer Horst Neisters giving a demonstration with his eagle at the 1976 Falconry Conference in Abu Dhabi.

exhibited, including books, illustrations and other informational material. The search was made in areas as far afield as Japan and the Americas. As a result an exhibition was mounted at the Conference site in which many comparatively rare items, including some going back to the mediaeval ages, when interest in falconry was at its zenith in Europe, were on show.

The Conference and Exhibition

The Conference gathered under an outsize Bedouin goat-hair tent in the vicinity of the Muqta Bridge which joins the island of Abu Dhabi to the mainland. The programme comprised sessions on the history of the sport, its past and present place in the world and methods of rearing birds and treating the ailments to which they are prone. Also discussed were hunting techniques and unethical behaviour incompatible with the reputation of a good falconer. His Highness Sheikh Sultan bin Zaid, the chairman of the Conference Planning Committee, gave an address, in which he hoped that the foundations of a World Falconry Organisation would be laid. The German falconer, Horst Neisters, reported on an electronic tracking device which can be carried by falcons, lessening the risk of loosing them. Conservation projects within Abu Dhabi were revealed by the Under Secretary of the Ministry of Information and Culture. The benefits of the Conference were threefold: it was instrumental in creating friendships between those in the Emirates and else where interested in falconry; on a scholarly level, the conference afforded scientists and specialists the chance to meet and exchange ideas; and finally, it enabled the Arabs to demonstrate the skill and sportsmanship used in their hunting methods.

COMPILED BY YAHYA BADR

NOTES

These two pictures have much in common, even though several centuries separate them! There has always been a fascination in training one of the fiercest and freest of living creatures to work in partnership with man.

172

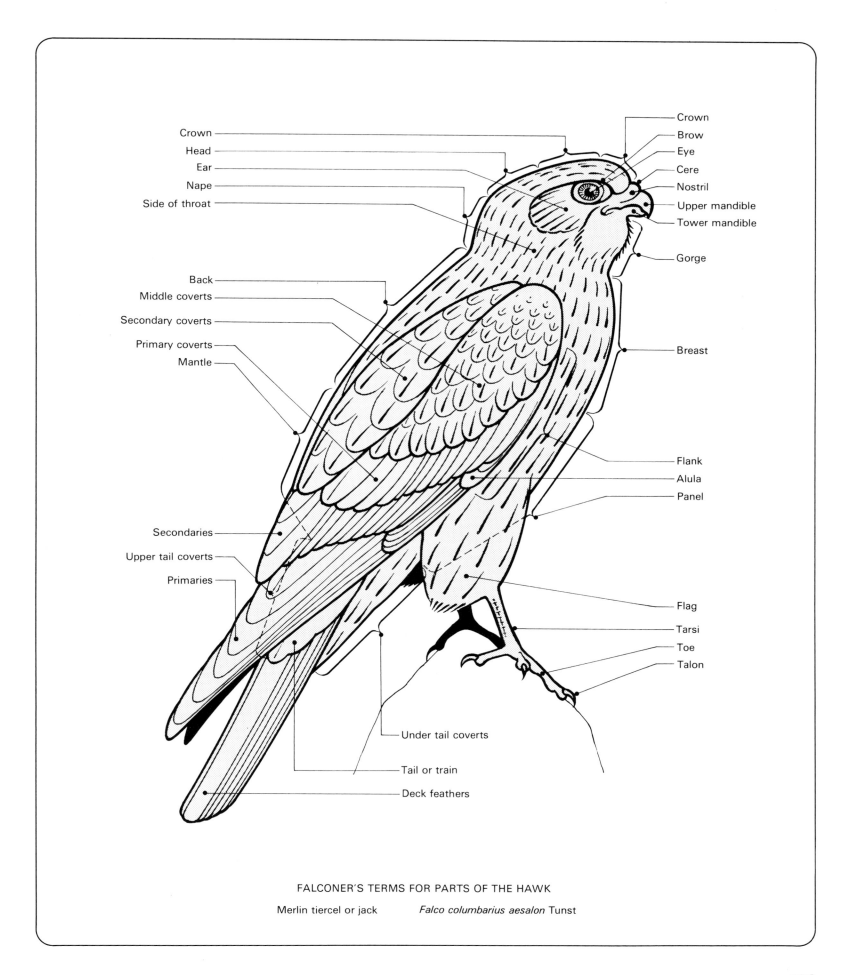

Crown
Head
Ear
Nape
Side of throat

Crown
Brow
Eye
Cere
Nostril
Upper mandible
Tower mandible

Gorge

Back
Middle coverts
Secondary coverts
Primary coverts
Mantle

Breast

Flank
Alula
Panel

Secondaries
Upper tail coverts
Primaries

Flag

Tarsi
Toe
Talon

Under tail coverts

Tail or train

Deck feathers

FALCONER'S TERMS FOR PARTS OF THE HAWK

Merlin tiercel or jack   *Falco columbarius aesalon* Tunst

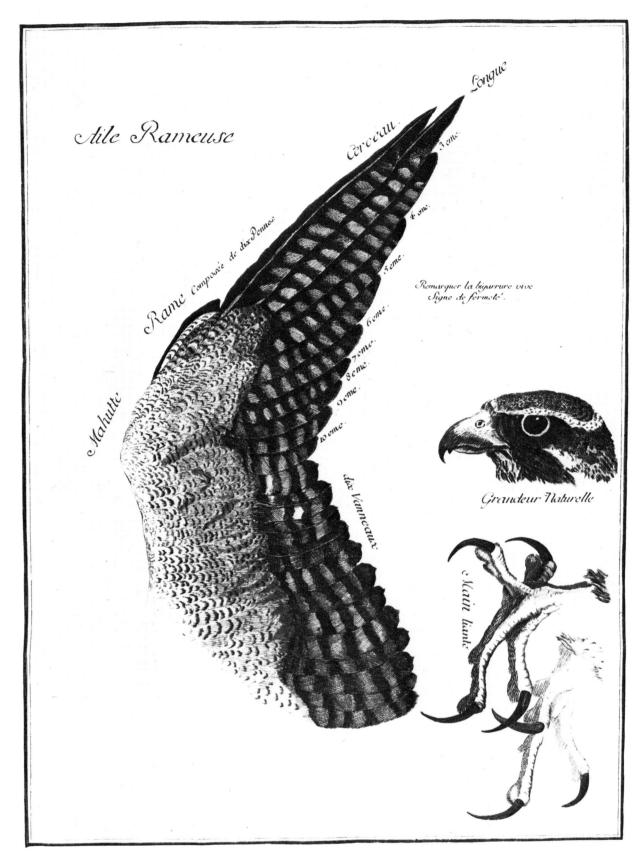

The illustrations on these two pages were taken from Huber's 'Observations sur le vol des oiseaux de proie', published in Geneva in 1784. The illustration above gives various anatomical details, while that on the right shows a classification of falcons and hawks into and low flyers.

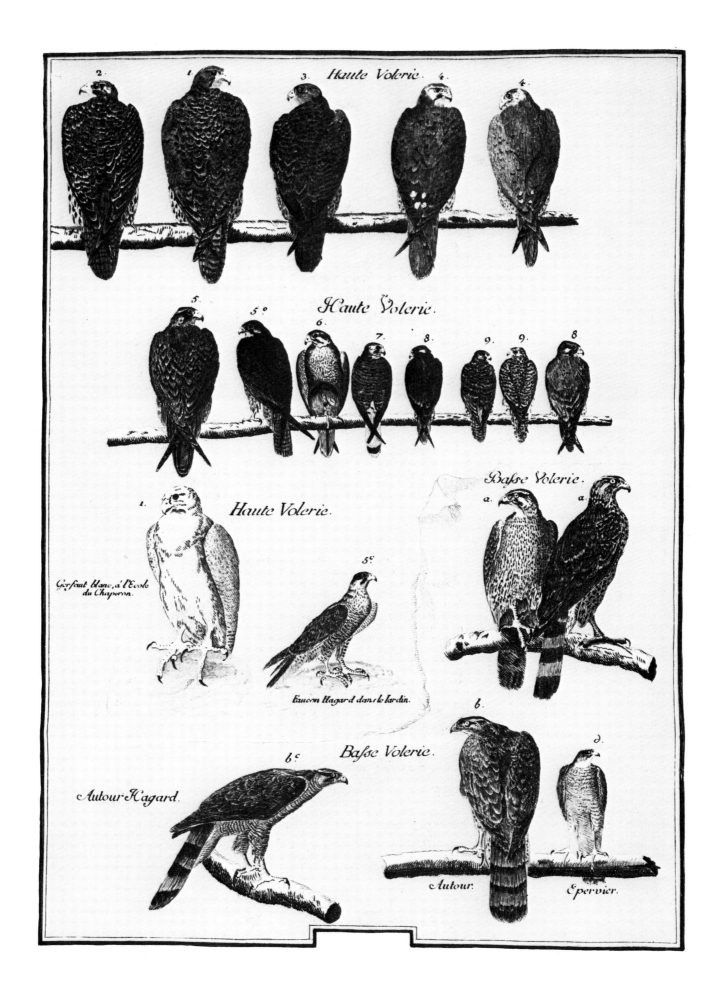

Haute Volerie.

Haute Volerie.

Haute Volerie.

Basse Volerie.

Gerfaut Blanc, à l'École du Chaperon.

Faucon Hagard dans le Jardin.

Autour Hagard.

Basse Volerie.

Autour.

Epervier.

Peregrine falcon *Falco peregrinus*

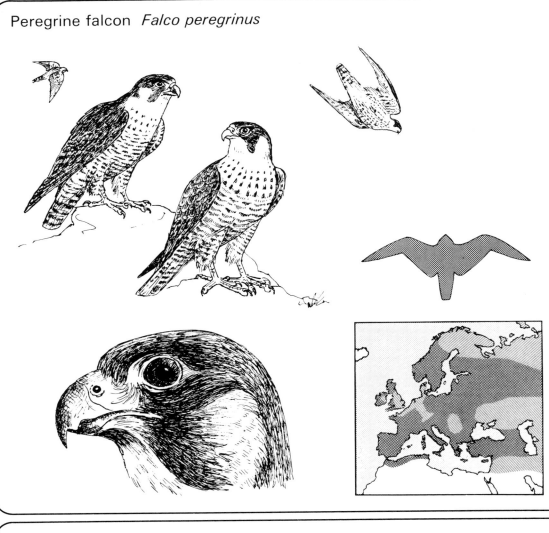

Characteristics:	medium to large-sized falcons, with broad black moustachial streaks (adult). Stocky bodies, short tails, sharply pointed, rather short wings. Barred underside.
Flight:	normal flight, quick short wingbeats, about 5-6 per second, interspersed with short glides. Average speed, level flight: 48-62 mph. Speed in stoop, about 85-87 mph.
Voice:	Alarm: hek-hek-hek, chick-ik, chick-ik at nest. Strill schreeeee-schreeee near nest.
Annual moult:	Generally April/September.

MALE

Length:	38 cm, wingspan 83 cm
Beak:	short, thick and curved, bluish
Wings:	sharply pointed, rather short
Colours:	crown, nape and back of neck bluish slate. Mantle, scapulars, back and upper-tail coverts blue-grey, barred darker slate. Breast buff, barred black, throat white, legs bright yellow.

FEMALE

Length:	48 cm, wingspan 113 cm
Colours:	much darker, spotted throat
Food:	chiefly birds up to the size of wild duck and small wild geese. Game birds, such as Red Grouse, francolins, and pigeons, especially Rock Doves. Rarely mammals. Occasionally frogs, insects, etc.

Goshawk *Accipiter gentilis*

	Present in spring and summer (nesting)
	Present all year round
	Present in winter only

Characteristics:	Large size, hawk-like proportions, and orange-red eyes.
Flight:	Capable of very fast short burst of speed, and is very manoeuvrable, weaving round trees with the aid of its long tail.
Habitat:	Forests, clearings in woods.
Voice:	High-pitched ca ca ca ca, or gek-gek-gek-gek, deeper and hoarser in female. Plaintive scream hi-aa given by female when male enters nest area.
Annual moult:	During summer months.

MALE

Length:	48 cm, wingspan 100 cm
Beak:	slim but strong, curved, slate-grey
Wings:	short and rounded
Tail:	very long
Colours:	centre of crown blackish-brown, sides of crown and eyebrows, fore-ear coverts and nape, whitish, steaked blackish-brown, mantle, back, upper-wing coverts and tail coverts, brown, tinged grey. Underside of tail and wing greyish-white barred dark brown. Legs yellow.

FEMALE

Length:	60 cm, wingspan 120 cm
Colours:	similar to male, but rather browner
Food:	large and medium-sized birds and mammals up to the size of Black Grouse or a young hare. Tree squirrels, and crows. In general, takes more mammals than most hawks.

Golden Eagle *Aquila ch. chrysaetos*

Characteristics:	Dark brown colour, very large size and graceful flight. Square tail, feathered tarsus.
Flight:	Graceful, soaring flight, glides sometimes averaging 40-60 mph. Sometimes vertical dives, which may attain 100 mph.
Habitat:	Mountains, uninhabited forests.
Voice:	Clear yelping call weeeo-hyo-hyo-hyo. Otherwise thin shrill pleek or tsewk.
Annual moult:	April to November.

MALE

Length:	75 cm, wingspan 188 cm
Weight:	3600 kg to 3750 kg
Beak:	long and hooked
Wings:	long and wide, with wide-spaced primaries
Colour:	Crown and nape feathers tipped and edged golden-buff or tawny. Whole rest of upper side, including upperwing coverts, dark brown. Underside from chin to belly brown, paler than upper side. Thighs paler. Feet yellow, bill and claws black.

FEMALE

Length:	83 cm, wingspan 230 cm
Weight:	4100 kg to 6000 kg
Colour:	similar to the male
Food:	preference for mammals, gamebirds, and carrion. Lizards and snakes, jays and crows, foxes, stoats, mink and dead fish.

European Sparrow-hawk *Accipiter nisus nis*

Characteristics:	One of the smaller hawks, male rather small.
Flight:	Capable of great speed for a short distance. Speed on migration 26 mph, and they may rise to 3000 feet. Very manoeuvrable in cover.
Habitat:	Hedges, copses, fields, the edge of woods.
Voice:	Normal call kek-kek-kek-kek. With food kew-kew-kew-kew, in rage of fear tirrr-tirrr.
Annual moult:	From May to August.

MALE

Length:	27 cm, wingspan 60 cm
Beak:	short and hooked
Wings:	short, rounded
Tail:	very long
Colour:	above, dark slate, long upper-tail coverts tipped white. Tail brown, washed slaty, tipped white, with narrow dark brown bars. Upper wing dark slate, tinged brown. Chin and throat white or buff, streaked dark brown. Rest of underside barred white. Eye bright yellow, feet yellow.

FEMALE

Length:	37 cm, wingspan 80 cm
Colour:	much browner than the male
Food:	largely small birds, from the size of a tit to a thrush. Sometimes larger, such as jays. Females can kill a wood pigeon. Rarely mammals, insects.

Bibliography

BEEBE and WEBSTER, *North American Falconry and Hunting Hawks,*   Denver 1964

BERNERS, Dame Julia, *Boke of St Albans,*   1486

BERT, Edmund, *Treatise on Hawks and Hawking,* .... London, 1619

BLAINE, Gilbert, *Falconry,* .... London, 1936

BLOME, Richard, *Hawking or Falconry,* .... London, 1929

EVANS, Humphrey Ap, *Falconry for You,* .... London, 1963

GLASIER, Phillip, *As the Falcon her Bells,* .... London, 1964
                  Falconry and Hawking, ... London, 1978

HOHENSTAUFEN, Frederick II of, *The Art of Falconry,* Stanford, Calif., 1943, 1961

ILLINGWORTH, Frank, *Falcons and Falconry,* .... London, 1948, 1968

LASCELLES, Hon. Gerald, *The Art of Falconry,* .... London, 1892, 1971

MAVROGORDATO, Jack, *A Hawk for the Bush,* .... Suffolk, 1960, 1973

PETERS, H. J. and JAMESON, E. W., *American Hawking,* .... Davis, Calif. 1970

SAMSON, Jack, *Falconry Today,* .... New York, 1976

THESINGER, Wilfred, *Arabian Sands,* .... London, 1959

WOODFORD, M. H., *A Manual of Falconry,* .... London, 1963

Colour plates

Photographic Credits